brandwatching

lifting the lid on branding

About the author

Giles Lury is a Murphy's-drinking, Toyota-driving, Lego-watch-wearing, Tesco-shopping (and Chelsea supporting) father of five. He is also Brand Consultancy Director at Springpoint Ltd.

He has over sixteen years experience in marketing and advertising, working on brands including Bird's Eye, British Airways, Cockburn's, Impulse, Monopoly, Oxo and Volkswagen.

He has written two award-winning papers for the IPA Advertising Effectiveness Awards and won the Gold Prize at The AMSO Research Effectiveness Awards with a paper he co-wrote.

His specialist subject, should he appear on Mastermind, would be "The life and times of the Oxo brand".

brandwatching

lifting the lid on branding

Giles Lury

BLACKHALL
Publishing

This book was typeset by
Gough Typesetting for

BLACKHALL PUBLISHING
8 Priory Hall, Stillorgan
Co. Dublin, Ireland

and

BLACKHALL PUBLISHING
2027 Hyperion Avenue
Los Angeles, CA 90027
USA

email: blackhall@eircom.net
website: www.blackhallpublishing.com

First published 1998
Second edition 2001

ISBN: 1 842180 25 8

A catalogue record for this book
is available from the British Library.

Printed in Ireland by
ColourBooks Ltd

For Karen
and our five brand extensions:
Rebecca, Jack, Callum, Theo and Ewan.

Contents

Acknowledgements

This may be the nearest I'll ever get to a Oscar acceptance speech but there are lots of people I do genuinely wish to thank.

Everyone at The Value Engineers and a number who are no longer 'engineers', including Thom Braun, Bruce Davis, Phil Spires, Beth Flynn, Anthony Hannant and Tess Wicksteed.

Everyone at Springpoint, but especially Roman Huszak for re-designing the cover.

Everyone at Blackhall Publishing for their help and encouragement with this book.

Rob and Margaret Allen and the late Norman Hart, for their respective hands in introducing me to Blackhall.

All my family who played their parts, Adam, Celia, Karen and her husband Tim Neil, but most especially to Karen, my wife, chief proofreader and sanity checker.

And finally to all those companies who have kindly given their permission for me to use pictures of their brands.

Thank you.

Giles Lury
July, 2001

The illustrations in this book are the trademarks and property of the individual companies concerned and are reproduced with their kind permission. The author and Blackhall Publishing would like to thank each of these companies for their co-operation in the reproduction of *Brandwatching*.

A A
Bird's Eye Wall Ltd
BMW
Britvic Soft Drinks
Cadbury Ireland Ltd
Coca-Cola limited
Colgate-Palmolive Ireland
General Mills
H J Heinz Company Ltd
HHCL + Partners
Interbrand
Kodak Ltd
Legoland Windsor Park Ltd
Lever Brothers Ltd
McDonald's Restaurants Ltd
Mercedez-Benz (United Kingdom) Ltd
Murphy Brewery Ireland Ltd
Nestlé Ireland Ltd
Orkla Brand School
Palyboy Enterprises Inc.
Procter & Gamble
R J Reynolds
Revlon International Corporation
SmithKline Beecham (Ireland) Ltd
The Body Shop International PLC
The Henley Centre
Trebor Bassett Ltd
Van den Bergh Foods
Virgin Enterprises Ltd
Welsh Tourist Board
WWF-UK Ltd

Introduction

The practice of branding, although over 2,000 years old, is primarily a 20th century phenomenon. I believe it is one of *the* most important phenomena of the century. It ranks with the decline of imperialism, the growth of feminism and the arrival of the atomic age.

It is perhaps only television, with its now universal ability to communicate, educate and entertain, that has had more impact. In today's increasingly market-led society it is often said that *'the consumer is king'* and while we consume products, it is brands we buy.

Branding is big, big business. In a recent survey, the top five brands in the world – Coca-Cola, Marlboro, IBM, McDonald's and Disney – were valued at a combined total of $222 billion! (and that's just the top five).

However, it is not just their financial size that demonstrates their potency and impact. Coca-Cola, in its distinctive red and white livery, is the most recognisable word in the world. The golden arches of McDonald's and Disney's fairy-tale castle are amongst the world's most famous icons. No longer are films, sport and music the only global themes. Brands span the world touching millions.

Every day of our lives, each and every one of us chooses and uses brands. Every house doesn't have *one*, every house contains hundreds of them. The house may even be branded itself – a Barrett or a Wimpey home. We make literally thousands of brand decisions every week. I'm thirsty, shall I have a Budweiser or a Guinness? I'm peckish, shall I have a Mars or a KitKat?

Indeed, an increasing number of observers believe that as more and more of the traditional social and cultural barriers break down it will be our role as consumers that will define who we are. We are what we eat, what we drink, what we wear, what we wash our hair with … 'brandographics' is replacing demographics and psychographics.

The influence of brands in our lives stretches well beyond that which stems from our direct purchase and consumption of them. They play a fundamental role in today's media rich world.

Commercial television and radio, newspapers and magazines rely on the revenue that brand advertising brings. Those little three-minute commercial breaks help pay for the twenty minutes of programming. The ads help fund the editorial. In a media world dominated by commercial concerns, brands are the paymasters behind the presenters. Indeed, as overtly sponsored television programmes arrive in the UK this is truer than ever.

But the influential effect of brands doesn't stop there. Brands are part of our lives, so they make news and they are legitimate material for scriptwriters and presenters. Brands have become part of our everyday language – "I'll just do the Hoovering" and created more recently "You've been Tango'd".

Brands are a regular source of material for comedians. Rory Bremner recently said of a fellow comic:

> Victoria Wood can locate areas of British life and humour, very sharply and very economically, with just a brand name or two.

Branding, however, is no joke. In a recent survey it was found that consumers believed that brands like Kellogg's, Cadbury's, Heinz, Nescafé and Rowntree were more likely to treat them honestly and fairly than any institution of British life except their GP. In other words, today's average consumer is more likely to trust Kellogg's than the Church!

In a further demonstration of the impact of brands and in an ironic turn of events we are increasingly paying to become walking advertisements for the brands we like. It may not be sensible to wear your heart on your sleeve but we are happy to wear our brands on our chests (and elsewhere) as the sales of overtly branded T-shirts, bags, sweatshirts and jumpers continue to soar. We, the consumers, are also the medium for the message and what's more we are paying for that privilege.

Perhaps the ultimate manifestation of the impact of branding was the neon advertising sign that greeted the return of America's first moon-walking astronauts. It read simply:

Welcome back to Earth, home of Coca-Cola.

This book explores the phenomena that is branding.

What is a brand?

O pen any fridge in the UK and, more likely than not, you will find at least one of the following: *Anchor* butter, *Flora* margarine or *Müller* yoghurt. Open the cupboards in the rest of the kitchen and again you shouldn't be in the least surprised to find at least one of *Kellogg's* corn flakes, *Nescafé* instant coffee, *McVitie's* digestive biscuits or *Heinz* tomato ketchup. In many households you will find all four of them.

Moving to the bathroom, you might well find *Colgate* or *Macleans* toothpaste and *Pantene* or *Organics* shampoo.

Finally into the bedroom, and in the underwear drawer it is almost certain that you will find at least one pair of *Marks & Spencer* knickers.

- ♦ What are these names, these so called brands?
- ♦ What makes them special?
- ♦ Why do we insist on, and persist in, buying them?

REGISTERED TRADE MARK

Coca-Cola is now the second most recognisable word in the world and consequently the world's most famous brand. If you believe it is just the name given to a cola 110 years ago by a company based in Atlanta Georgia, then you are greatly underestimating the power of branding.

While dictionary definitions of 'brand' reflect the origins of branding with reference to distinctive marks on cattle, most also include the more modern interpretation of a name given to a specific product or service by a company.

> **brãnd**   n. *burning or charred log or stick, (poet.) torch,*
> *(– from the burning, rescued person, convert);*
> *permanent mark deliberately made by hot iron; stigma*
> *(– of Cain, blood-guilt); trade mark, goods of particular*
> *make or trade mark (lit. or fig.); iron stamp for burning-*
> *in mark; (poet.) sword; kind of blight in which leaves*
> *look burnt; - -new conspicuously or completely new. [*
> *OE, = OHG brant, ON brandr f. Gmc * brandaz (*bran-*
> *BURN)]*

> *Concise Oxford English Dictionary*

Philip Kotler in his definitive marketing textbook, *Managing Markets: Planning, Analysis and Control*, defines a brand as follows:

> *A name, term, symbol or design, or a combination of*
> *them which is intended to signify the goods or services*
> *of one seller or group of sellers and to differentiate them*
> *from those of competitors.*

However, these definitions with their emphasis on names or trademarks are really inadequate for today's highly developed consumer society and today's marketing literate consumers. Sir Michael Perry, a former Chairman of Unilever, the company that owns brands such as Persil, Birds Eye, PG Tips and Calvin Klein said recently:

> *In the modern world, brands are a key part of how*
> *individuals define themselves and their relationships*
> *with one another. . . More and more we are simply*
> *consumers. . . We are what we wear, what we eat, what*
> *we drive.*

Brands, as Sir Michael Perry and millions of us consumers know, are much more than the sum of their physical parts. Coca-Cola is much more than a name, it is much more than a sweet, fizzy, brown drink made from vegetable extracts. Coca-Cola is a way of life.

Brands are a whole bundle of attributes, both functional and emotional. Coca-Cola is refreshing but it is also young, lively and energetic.

Brands have personalities; they have and represent certain values. Brands not only meet our physical needs, they can address our emotional needs too. They make a statement about the type of person you are or would like to be.

Stephen King was Director of Planning at one of the world's largest advertising agencies, J Walter Thompson, when he wrote a seminal paper entitled *"What is a brand?"* In it, he too argued that while a brand has values as a product it also has values beyond the physical or functional ones.

> *People choose their brands as they choose their friends. You choose your friends not usually because of specific skills or physical attributes (though of course these come into it) but simply because you like them as people. It is the total person you choose, not a compendium of virtues and vices.*

This might perhaps be thought a rather fanciful way of describing why one brand is valued more than another. But it is not too hard to find evidence to support it, for instance, 'blind' versus 'named' product tests.

In this type of test, two matched samples of consumers are each asked to try and then rate two products. One sample tries the two products 'blind' – that is they are not told what the brands are – while the other sample are told which product is which brand. It is then possible to compare the results and see the effect that branding has on perception. Here is an example from the Stephen King paper. The two well-known brand names have been replaced by letters A and B for reasons of confidentiality.

Blind v Named Product Test: Food Product		
	Blind	Named
Brand A	49%	33%
Brand B	51%	67%
(percentage preferring overall, excludes don't knows)		

Brands A and B appear to be level on physical, functional performance but Brand B has considerably more 'added values'.

What this test shows is that, when tested blind, consumers are equally split between the two products. Functionally there is little, if anything, the people can perceive to choose between the two. However, when consumers are told in advance the names of the products, a majority state a preference for Brand B.

Clearly there is something about Brand B as a *brand* which raises its value over that of Brand A. It cannot be a physical or functional thing since that would have shown up in the blind test. Therefore it has to be assumed that Brand B offers the consumer something more than Brand A – some form of non-functional added value.

In a more recent blind test Coca-Cola was tested against Pepsi and, despite the fact that Coca-Cola sells much more than Pepsi, Pepsi was the clearly preferred cola when tested blind.

So it is clear that brands are much more than names. They are more than physical entities: much of what we see and value in them exists in our minds and not in the products themselves. It is our perceptions – our beliefs and our feelings – about a brand that are most important.

The true meaning and power of branding exists in the minds of you and me and not in the products themselves. Sir Charles Revlon realised this when he said of his brand:

> *In the factory we make cosmetics, in the store we sell hope.*

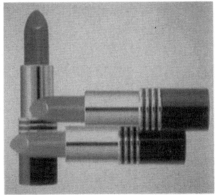

What are the origins of branding?

While the word 'branding' is linked with the cowboys of the old Wild West, there are many earlier examples of owners or manufacturers marking their property and produce with a distinctive and distinguishing symbol or name. Some of the earliest examples of these 'trademarks' are 9000 years old.

It's not hard to imagine why branding has been around for centuries. By marking your products, you would be labelling your goods as your property or the fruits of your labour. Any potential purchaser seeing your mark could identify you as its producer or owner.

Then, over time, as more and more people bought your products, your mark or name might establish a reputation for itself. It would have become associated with certain standards. Your 'brand' would have started to establish its own unique set of values.

According to Thomas Hine in his book, *The Total Package*, the earliest known example of a true branded product was the 'Fortis' oil-burning lamp from Roman times. It was produced in Lombardy up until the 2nd century AD when it was apparently replaced by cheaper imitations.

However it was the 19th century that arguably saw the dawn of the modern branding era and it was the industrial revolution that caused its birth. It was the industrial revolution that created the mass production that meant an ever increasing proportion of people worked for a manufacturer and not themselves. They no longer needed to mark the products they produced as their own, rather what they produced was collectively produced for one company.

The ensuing rapid raising standards of living led to the creation of the first mass-markets – people who were no longer self-sufficient but who had money and were in the market for goods.

Then there was mass distribution. Until the rise of the railways the only mass distribution of goods was undertaken by ship or barge and while this did mean that some trade in branded goods grew up around ports and their hinterlands their influence was limited. The railways especially in countries like the USA facilitated the shipments of goods around the country on a much wider scale. Mass production would never really have taken off without mass distribution to get the goods to the different markets in the different towns and cities.

Finally it was the growth of education and literacy that accompanied the industrial revolution that created the fourth key factor behind the birth of branding – the mass media through which manufacturers could communicate and sell their goods to the mass market – the consumers.

Wally Olins, co-founder and Chairman of leading British design company, Wolff Olins, described the process in his book *Corporate Identity*:

> *The idea of branding emerged in the middle of the 19th century, when technology combined with literacy and rising standards of living to create the first mass market.*
>
> *The thinking that lay behind branding was very simple, but highly original. It was to take a household product, a commodity, not different fundamentally from any other made by another manufacturer, and to endow it with special characteristics through the imaginative use of name, packaging and advertising.*
>
> *The companies, mainly American, that originated the branded idea all began in more or less the same way. They took ordinary, standard products, such as soap or tea, coffee or fats, and they gave them a distinctive name and packaging. They advertised them very heavily and then they distributed them widely. The achievement of those companies was prodigious. They took advantage of the latest technology available at the time, rapid, regular and widespread transport, refrigeration, cheap newspapers, mass advertising to reach a public with improved living standards.*

This process of taking a product, giving it a distinctive name and attractive packaging and then advertising it to highlight its merits and/or create a personality for it, is the basis for one of the traditional and most widely used explanations of what a brand is. For many people a brand is a product to which the marketer has added special values or characteristics.

However, the origins of branding was not, as Wally Olins suggests, just some early marketer's clever ploy dependent on an original name, a flashy pack and smart advertising (although they undoubtedly helped). Those early brands offered their consumers a real benefit.

The reliability and consistency of product quality was a persistent problem for consumers in the 19th century. Branding was the means by which this problem was addressed and resolved (as the history of Sunlight soap related by Sir Michael Perry former chairman of Unilever demonstrates):

When William Hesketh Lever first packaged up his Sunlight soap, he had a clear sense of what he was offering to Lancashire housewives. It was a reassuring guarantee of predictability and consistency. It wasn't possible for the housewife to get the equivalent guarantee elsewhere.

Certainly not when she purchased a lump of soap which had been cut off a block of unknown origin and uncertain quality in a grocer's store. William Hesketh Lever's simple brand guarantee was a foundation of a world-wide integrated business – from the palm tree to the soap kettle as he put it.

Explained like this it is clear that branding was not just a wheeze. It provided a reassuring guarantee of predictability and consistency for the consumer. It wasn't possible for that customer to get the equivalent guarantee elsewhere. Traditionally they had bought products of "unknown origin and uncertain quality" which might have been exposed to anything in the store. Even if they had bought a product and liked it once, they had no guarantee that it would be the same when they went back to buy it again.

This early advertisement for Uneeda biscuits, quoted in Thomas Hine's *The Total Package*, further highlights some of the potential problems that consumers might face when buying an unbranded product.

> *The Grocer couldn't help it.*
>
> *When the grocery boy swept out the store, he couldn't find the lid of the cracker box, so he covered them over with a codfish crate. After he weighed a mackerel and drew a quart of kerosene, he filled an order for a pound of crackers, which was carefully picked from the cracker box under the codfish crate. The customer who bought the crackers said they tasted queer, but the grocer couldn't help it.*

Brands, with their superior packaging and their promise of consistent high standards, could offer a persuasive alternative – an easily recognisible and reassuring guarantee of quality.

This was to prove a strong basis on which brands could be built and indeed many of today's famous brands can trace their roots back to this period. In his book, *How it all Began*, Maurice Baren has chronicled the histories behind many famous brands and shown how some can trace their roots back to the 19th century.

He notes that it was in 1824 that John Cadbury first opened a store but interestingly at that time the sale of tea, coffee, cocoa and *chocolate* was only a sideline.

♦ Robert McVitie set up business at 150 Rose Street, Edinburgh in a house owned by his father. The year was 1830.

♦ Beecham can trace its origins back to 1840 when Thomas Beecham first began to roll and powder pills.

♦ It was in 1876 that an American, Henry Heinz, persuaded his brother, John, and his cousin, Frederick, to put up enough money to launch the F & J Heinz Company with Henry as its first manager. By 1888, Henry had bought out both Frederick and John and re-named the firm H J Heinz Company.

♦ On the 8 May 1886 a new brand went on sale at Jacob's Pharmacy in Atlanta. The brand was none other than Coca-Cola.

Later the same year, on 3 November in fact, in an area of New Zealand called Waikato, the first Anchor butter was churned.

♦ The final decade of the 19th century was obviously a time for brand-loving sweet eaters as all of the following confectioneries were launched: Rowntree's Fruit Pastilles (1891), Rowntree's Fruit Gums, Wrigley's Juicy Fruit and Spearmint Gum (all 1893) and Bassett's Liquorice Allsorts (1899).

The last of these is said to have been 'invented' as the result of an accident when a Bassett's salesman, named Charlie Thompson, knocked over several of his sample boxes. The resulting 'mix' was more appealing than any of the individual products to Charlie's prospective buyer and 'Allsorts' were born. (See the colour section.)

Only a few brands have been created by accident but 'brands' have been created in their thousands for hundreds of years and branding shows every sign of continuing into the next millennium.

3

Are there different types of branding?

From its humble origins, where most brand names stood for one product being produced by one company, branding has become much bigger and more complex. Nowadays there are many, many different types of brands and, with marketers' inherent love of jargon, a whole myriad of branding terms to go with them. There are:

- *product brands and range brands;*
- *manufacturer, retailer and service brands;*
- *pillar brands and power brands;*
- *company and corporate brands;*
- *superbrands and sub-brands.*

To make matters worse, there is no general agreement as to the exact definition of all these different types of brands. To make matters downright confusing, one product can now have a number of different levels of branding.

This hierarchy of branding has itself been given a label – it is known as 'brand architecture'. Graham Harding, Managing Director of The Value Engineers says:

> *The purpose of brand architecture is to make life simple for the consumer and difficult for the competition.*

But also wryly notes that:

> *. . . it often confuses the consumer and makes life easy for the competition.*

What follows below is, therefore, a brief attempt to introduce and explain some of the different types of branding that exist today.

In the beginning, branding tended to be fairly straightforward. There was a product which was given a name. This name was often the name of its inventor or creator. Furthermore that name was also the name given to the company that produced it. Take for example, Mars.

Forrest E Mars came to Britain in 1932 bringing with him the recipe for a new type of confectionery bar which was made with chocolate, nougat and caramel. He gave it its, or rather his, name – the Mars bar – and the company that produced it was also, not too surprisingly, named after him.

It rapidly became an example of what is generally known as a 'product or individual brand'. In other words, it was a brand that was a single product type in a single market.

However, as markets have become more and more competitive over the years, brands and branding have developed. Like many other brands, variations on the original Mars theme of nougat, caramel and *"thick, thick chocolate"* have been created. For example you can now buy Kingsize Mars and Mars Miniatures but as these are still basically the same type of product in the same 'chocolate confectionery' market, it does not change how Mars would be classified by most marketers. It will still be a product brand.

However, as nowadays you can also buy a Mars Ice Cream and a Mars Milk Drink, the Mars brand is no longer offering just one type of product, but a whole range of different products that compete in different markets – the chocolate confectionery market, the ice cream market and the flavoured milk market.

Mars would therefore normally be classified as a 'range or family brand'.

The Mars company has also developed over the years. It is no longer the name of a company that produces only the Mars range.

Mars is now one of the largest confectionery companies in the world. It has a number of other confectionery brands (some of which are product brands and some of which are range brands!). They include Snickers, Bounty, Opal Fruits (now Starburst), Maltesers, M&Ms and Galaxy.

What's more, Mars the company also owns other brands in other markets like Dolmio, the Italian-food range brand and Pedigree, the leading dog food range brand.

The Mars brand name doesn't appear on the front or even the back of many of these other brands so their brand architecture is not confused in any way by getting into the realms of multiple branding.

However, if we take another example from the confectionery market it's immediately clear that this isn't always the case. Let's look at KitKat.

This brand, at first glance, could perhaps be said to be schizophrenic. It is two brands in one. Like Mars, KitKat started life as a product brand but now with the introduction of different sizes, flavours and KitKat ice creams it would be a 'range brand'.

However KitKat isn't just KitKat, it is also branded 'Nestlé'. Nestlé is the company that now owns KitKat (having bought Rowntree-Macintosh). Nestlé is a 'company or house or umbrella brand' meaning it is a company (or 'house') that uses its name across a range of different brands and products. It is the umbrella under which all of them 'nestle'.

So what sort of brand is KitKat? Well, in fact, what many marketers would classify it as is a 'house-endorsed range brand'.

KitKat is the 'heart' of the brand. It is the name the vast majority of people like you and me will know and associate with the product. Nestlé plays a secondary role, it acts as a further reassurance of quality for those people who notice it and who know who Nestlé are. It is perhaps more appropriate to think of the true branding to be 'KitKat from Nestlé'. Rather than schizophrenic, 'KitKat from Nestlé' is just a more complex form of brand architecture.

With the increasing concentration of business into a smaller number of companies there are nowadays many brands that are endorsed by a house or family brand. Some like KitKat, are only endorsed at a low level while, for others, the house branding is more important.

One market where this practice is prevalent is the motor industry where the individual product brands are often subordinate to the overall house brand or marque. For example, Volkswagen is the dominant brand for Volkswagen Polo. Polo is often then called the 'sub-brand'.

In fact it is possible to plot a continuum of these different models of branding architecture ranging from those that are house brand focused to those that are product/range brand focused.

- *House brand focused:*
  where the complete focus of branding is on the house brand.
  Examples include ICI, BMW and Burberry's.
- *House brand led:*
  where any product or range brand is subordinate to the house brand.
  Examples include Volkswagen (Polo) and Ford (Escort).
- *House brand – product brand equality:*
  where the house brand and any product or range brand play an equally important role in the total brand.
  Examples include L'Oréal Studioline.
- *House brand endorsed product or range brand:*
  where the product or range brand plays the lead or dominant role in the branding but the house brand plays a subservient role as a quality endorsement.
  Examples include Nestlé KitKat and Lever Persil.
- *Product brand focused:*
  where the house brand plays no role in the branding.
  Examples include Ariel and Pampers (both Procter & Gamble) and Linda McCartney (United Biscuits).

Different companies adopt different policies and practices,

and while this spectrum is useful in helping to analyse what any brand is doing at one point in time, few things remain constant and over a period of time different brands evolve and change.

One example which reflects a recent trend to greater emphasis on house branding would be 'Persil from Lever' – originally a product brand but now a 'house brand-endorsed range brand'!!!

Persil can trace its roots right back to the beginning of this century and the works of Professor Glessier and Dr Bauer of Stuttgart. Together they produced a new soap containing a bleaching agent and named it after two of its key ingredients PER-borate and SIL-icate. The soap, or rather the infant brand, was sold to a company called Crosfields in 1909. Then in 1919, Crosfields was bought by Lever Bros Ltd.

The now famous "Persil washes whiter" advertising theme was launched in the early days of the Second World War and, as those early ads demonstrated, this was a true product brand with no reference or endorsement from any house brand.

The brand continued to prosper and in 1968, a biological Persil was launched. Later, it was followed by Persil Automatic. The brand was adapting to the changing times and the changing needs of its consumers. Then in 1990 the brand extended into the washing up market with the launch of Persil Washing Up Liquid, taking on the dominant Fairy Liquid brand. With this move the brand became a range brand.

Another change had also taken place by the end of the 1980s. Lever had been introduced explicitly as a house brand endorsement. It appeared on the front of the pack and in the advertising.

Now Persil was and is a large and powerful brand with a loyal base of users. It didn't really need endorsement from what was a virtually unknown house brand. The fact that Persil was made by Lever added little or nothing to the brand's appeal in the eyes of its consumers. Why then was it done?

The answer lies not in looking at it from Persil's point of view but rather from understanding what the house brand, Lever, might gain. What Lever aimed to do was build awareness of its brand name and get it associated with its complete portfolio of brands. A portfolio that includes not only Persil, but also Surf, Comfort, Radion and Sunlight Soap. Lever would then become known as a company that produces good quality 'washing' products.

This would allow Lever to exploit its own name in two ways.

♦ Firstly, it could use Lever as a genuine endorsement of quality on any new brand it wanted to launch, giving that brand a 'running start'. The idea at its most basic was that the consumers would think: "Lever make Persil and those other good quality brands so new brand X which is also made by them should be good too. I'll give it a try."

♦ Secondly, with the cost of advertising increasing rapidly, there were an increasing number of occasions when it would be more cost efficient for Lever to advertise on behalf of all its brands rather than paying for each brand to advertise the same message separately.

One example of this would be the campaign Lever ran to inform its customers that it doesn't make any products for any of the retailers – an important message relevant to all its brands and their consumers (see page 17).

There is one final form of brand classification that is important to recognise when discussing modern brands and that is the distinction between manufacturer brands, service brands and retailer brands.

Coming back to our original example of Mars, we can define it as a 'manufacturer brand'. Mars, the company, produces or manufactures its own products which it then sells through a

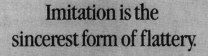

Imitation is the sincerest form of flattery.

And although we enjoy the flattery, we hope you're not fooled by the imitations.

The only place you'll find New System Persil Automatic powder is in a New System Persil Automatic pack. That's because New System Persil Automatic is made by Lever, which means it's only ever sold under the Lever name. Just like all the other famous Lever names on this page.

So take care our imitators don't soft soap you into believing otherwise.

LEVER

made for you and nobody else.

variety of channels to us, the consumers.

This contrasts with a 'service brand', which is a brand (and often a company) that offers a service to customers and competes in a service industry, such as banking or insurance (examples include Barclays, Britannia Building Society and British Gas).

Then there is a 'retailer brand', which is a brand (and again often a company) whose primary business function is not in making but in selling products or services (examples include Tesco, Sainsbury's and Marks & Spencer).

Many retailers brands therefore sell other companies' brands. You can buy Persil, Oxo and Kellogg's Corn Flakes at Tesco's. However, a number of these retailers also source products from manufacturers and brand it under their own name. This is known as 'own label' or perhaps more accurately as a 'retailers' own brand'. The success of retailers' own brands has been one of the most significant marketing phenomena of the last 20 years.

So, in conclusion, it is clear that there are many different types of brands and even more pieces of jargon to define them. If that wasn't difficult enough, not only can one product be multiple branded, it can, over time, change what type of brand it is!

Bird's Eye – World Cuisine – from MenuMaster is just one example of a confusing and confused brand architecture. (See the colour section.)

4

Why do we buy brands?

Many leading brands are anything from 25 per cent to 100 per cent more expensive than a retailer's own brand equivalent or an alternative named, but unknown, product. However, many of us still persist in buying the branded offer. We happily pay a significant price premium, time after time after time.

In fact, in May 1996 in the UK, it was possible to buy a 420g can of baked beans for 3p in some supermarkets. This compared with a price of 33p for an identically sized can of Heinz Baked Beans in the same shop. Heinz's Baked Beans were therefore *eleven* times more expensive than the retailer's own label equivalent yet lots of people were still buying Heinz beans.

Why do we persist in our desire for brands?

Perhaps the most obvious reason is that the Heinz beans are perceived to be better quality than their cheaper competitors. Brands have traditionally been, and remain, symbols of quality. As discussed earlier the origin of modern branding was as an easily recognisable mark of consistent quality.

It is clear that, over time, brands have gained a great deal of respect and trust in the eyes of the consumer. Indeed, in a recent survey conducted by The Henley Centre as part of its "Planning for Social Change" research programme, more

people trusted Kellogg's to be honest and fair than trusted
the Church.

In fact, the only British institution to beat the leading
brands on this measure of trust was the family GP! 85 per
cent of people said they trusted their GP to be honest and
fair, 84 per cent felt the same way about Kellogg's, while
only 64 per cent said the same thing about their church. (See
table 1 below.)

Perhaps not surprisingly MPs performed very badly with
only 28 per cent of people in the UK trusting their MP to be
honest and fair.

Table 1: Top brands beat Institutions on Trust

Percentage trusting the following to be honest and fair	
Your GP	85
Kellogg	84
Cadbury	83
Heinz	81
Nescafé	77
Rowntree	74
Your bank	72
Coca-Cola	65
Your church	64
The police	62
Your MP	28
	Source:*Henley Centre Planning for Social Change*

However, having said that brands are well respected and
trusted, it is equally true that brands no longer have it all
their own way. One of the most significant developments in
consumer marketing of the last 20 years has been the growth
of retailers' own label brands. Nowadays, in most grocery
markets, 25 per cent or more of the sales are to the retailers'
own label equivalents.

Britain leads the way in this own label phenomenon.
According to the research agency, A C Nielsen, who monitor
grocery sales across Europe, own label's share of the value of
grocery sales in 1993 was 27 per cent in Britain, 25 per cent
in Switzerland and 24 per cent in Germany. Figures for the

southern European countries where the retailers are much less developed are much lower – only 7.7 per cent in Italy and 8.1 per cent in Spain.

Sir Michael Perry, ex-Chairman of Unilever, described this transformation in a speech to the Advertising Association in 1994.

> *We no longer associate all supermarkets with the volume discounter's philosophy of "pile 'em high and sell 'em cheap". That is just one positioning. And the retailer that invented it no longer claims it.*
>
> *Stores like Sainsbury, Tesco and Safeway have established their own reputation as guarantors of freshness and quality – and far more than that. For enhancing enjoyment of shopping; for broadening the minds and experiences of their customers and for catering successfully to all incomes, classes and tastes. They have established powerful brand identities of their own which command consumer respect.*
>
> *This formidable achievement has inevitably changed the competitive context for the manufacturers' brands in those stores.* ***Consistency of quality is no longer enough. It's the minimum price of entry – but it's no guarantee you'll even get on the shelf.***

So, if the quality of retailers' own brands is now often as good if not better than the manufacturers' brands, as the results from numerous surveys show, why do we still persist in buying manufacturers' brands?

The answer lies in the fact that the quality of a brand only relates to its ability to physically do something for us. Philip Kotler, in *Marketing Management: Planning, Analysis and Control*, defines quality thus:

> *Quality stands for the rated ability of the brand to perform its functions. Quality is a summary term for the product's durability, reliability, precision, ease of repair and other valued attributes. Some of these attributes can be measured objectively.*

In other words quality relates to the functional benefit that a product offers. However (as we have seen in chapter one) we, the consumer, often respond to our own perceptions of quality, not any true measure of quality. Which in turn highlights the real reason why brands still have appeal for us.

We are not only driven by our rational needs. We have emotional needs as well as functional ones. We have hearts as well as minds and it is by addressing our emotional needs, as well as our functional needs, that a brand can create, not only its uniqueness, but its desirability. Sir Michael Perry again:

> *At the heart of the matter is the psychology of human emotions – like pride and self-regard. We all behave differently at different times when different considerations are at stake.*

> *It might depend on the perception of need at the time of purchase. For example a mother buying a fizzy drink might opt for a retailer's own brand for the noisy anonymity of a children's party – but **not** to accompany her on a highly visible school picnic where everyone is going to notice.*

Brands not only deliver functional benefits. They stand for certain values. They have their own personalities. They are a means of self-expression. These emotionally based factors can add to a brand's worth or at least our perception of its worth.

Take another example. You can put on a pair of anonymous trainers that have been designed and made to enhance your performance or you could put on a pair of Nike Air Trainers with the now unmistakable 'Swoosh' logo proudly displayed. The Nike trainers may or may not be better than the anonymous alternative but the Nike pair have their own style, their own character. They have what the Americans would call 'attitude'. They have a whole host of associations not least with top sports stars like Michael Jordan, Tiger Woods and Eric Cantona.

We may never be able to play like these world famous athletes but we like to be associated with them. We like and admire their attitude and style. We like the 'Just do it!' attitude of Nike. We like to feel that everyone else is wearing Nike trainers too. We want to be part of that 'brand tribe' – we want to belong to that club.

All of these are factors in how we make our choice and all of them help justify the price premium that Nike charges. They are not all rational. We may not even admit that they affect our decision but these emotional factors can have as much, if not more, influence that on a product's ability to deliver on functional grounds.

It's not that functional, rational factors are irrelevant – they are important, vitally important, it's just that fortunately for brand owners, humans are funny creatures and sometimes we do things that aren't completely logical.

Not surprisingly there have been many attempts to explain the appeal of branding but there is no simple foolproof model. However, it is clear that the complicated psychology of the human mind has a part to play.

Abraham Maslow, an eminent American psychologist, created what he called a 'Hierarchy of Needs' in an attempt to explain why different people will do different things at different times.

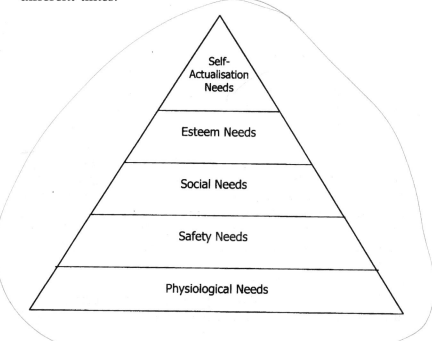

Maslow believed that people have a hierarchy of needs that starts with the most basic human needs for food, drink, heat and shelter. These are the most fundamental physical and functional human needs. As these basic needs are satisfied we progress up the hierarchy and the needs become more emotional and psychological. At the very top, is the wonderfully American notion of 'Self-actualisation needs', the need for self-development and self-realisation.

Against this model it is possible to look at brands and analyse how, in their own small and particular ways, they stack up against this hierarchy. At their most basic, brands perform a function for their consumers – Persil helps get your clothes clean.

However, a brand's image and personality, which is based on such factors as its name, how it is packaged, the way it is promoted and advertised, the values it projects, all encourage you to believe it also says something about you to others. It says something to friends, neighbours, strangers. It addresses your need for a social image. Your choice of brands also says something about you to yourself. It might be "I'm being a good mother" or "I'm in with the in-crowd". Brands therefore can be seen to address your need for a self-image too.

For years, Persil promoted itself via the 'Persil Mum' as a brand for people who are caring and loving yet efficient and reliable. At the heart of its appeal was the promise of "caring whiteness".

Persil's offer was based on a powerful combination of a basic emotional benefit – caring – and the functional benefit of clean clothes. So in other words, by choosing and using Persil the consumers not only got clean clothes they were projecting an image of themselves as good, sensible yet loving 'Mums' whilst saying to themselves that they were caring people. At least that is the theory!

Another theory often quoted to help explain people's choices is the Herzberg Theory of Motivation. Frederick Herzberg's theory identifies two key influences – *dissatisfiers* (those factors that cause dissatisfaction) and *satisfiers* (those factors that give or cause satisfaction). For example the lack of nutritional information on a pack of Fish Fingers might be a dissatisfier while the fact that they are made from fish fillet and not minced fish is likely to be a satisfier.

Dissatisfiers are not fundamental to the satisfaction of a brand and they certainly don't help sell it, in fact they can discourage sales. On the other hand satisfiers provide qualities or attributes that are key to the enjoyment and satisfaction a brand provides. They help sell the brand, they help motivate people to buy one particular brand instead of another.

The obvious conclusions are that any manufacturer should try to avoid any dissatisfiers and concentrate on identifying and providing the major satisfiers or motivators in the market.

However, in the context of real-life modern marketing and branding, this theory has been evolved a step further into a new and different two factor theory. Instead of dissatisfiers and satisfiers there are *motivators* and *discriminators*.

Modern marketers tend to focus on the positive and therefore they don't concentrate on, and certainly don't talk about, the negatives of their brand. They, like Michael Palin on the cross in the film *The Life of Brian*, are encouraged to *"always look on the bright side of life"*. It may be a cliché but marketers really are told not to look at anything as a problem but rather to look at it as an opportunity.

So to an extent they ignore the notion of dissatisfiers and put their efforts into satisfiers which they subdivide into motivators and, vitally important to the creation of a brand, discriminators. Motivators are the market generic benefits, the things that a brand must have if it wants to be considered – for example all lagers are 'refreshing'. On the other hand discriminators are those benefits or attributes that uniquely distinguish a brand and help provide the final reason for purchase. These can be functionally based but are often emotional or psychological benefits. Indeed they can be purely image based. Budweiser positions itself as 'The King of Beers', the genuine beer of the American people that is brewed over beechwood. (A rich mixture of functional and emotionally discriminating attributes.)

As mentioned earlier, there is no single model which explains why people choose brands but even this brief look at two of the most famous theories provides some insights. Indeed it is possible to merge and simplify the theories of Maslow and Herzberg and create a three level model that tries to incorporate some of the best elements of both theories.

The Three Levels for Brand Choice

Rational   *Motivators*
                                              (for getting
                                              considered)

1. Performance
Will it do or give me what I want?

2. Self-Image
What does it say to me about myself?

3. Social Image
What does it say to others about me?

Emotional   *Ultimate*
                                              Discriminators
                                              (Reasons for
                                              final purchase)

Source: *The Value Engineers*

No theory could rightly claim to capture and explain all the wonderful idiosyncrasies of the consumers' minds but it is undoubtedly true that we, those consumers, buy brands because they are much more than the sum of their physical parts. Our choice is not just based on what brands are *physically*, nor simply on what they *functionally* do for us.

We choose them because they offer us much more than purely tangible benefits. They offer us a whole bundle of attributes and benefits which address both our rational and our subjective, emotional needs.

The core of a brand's appeal lies in our perception of the unique combination of attributes it offers to us. Brands, quite simply, appeal to our minds *and* our hearts and that is why we continue to buy them.

5

What are brand managers and what do they do?

Many people have noted a similarity between Hollywood stars and famous brands – both should be unique and both should hold a special appeal for their 'viewing' or 'buying' public.

David Lamb, while Marketing Director of Rowntree-Macintosh, defined a 'star brand' as:

> . . . a product with a total aura of personality and complementing 'added values' which distinguish it from the mass of other products. . .The true brand is irreplaceable. It creates a uniqueness a competitor can never emulate.

He could have been describing any one of a number of Hollywood stars. There will only ever be one John Wayne, there will only ever be one Bette Davies, there will only ever be one Mars bar. However, behind the great Hollywood stars of the 1930s, 1940s and 1950s was the powerful and well-oiled Hollywood system and the stars' managers.

Clark Gable, the 'king' of Hollywood and a star for nearly 30 years was launched three times before he became an 'overnight success'. For the successful third launch, he was the romantic male lead complete with gruff 'machoness', a sense of humour, a moustache and an impudent grin. Having found a winning formula his manager ensured that Clark Gable appeared in a string of roles opposite the likes of Jean Harlow, Carole Lombard and, most famously, Vivien Leigh in *Gone with the Wind*.

Each time he was a romantic lead, complete with gruff machoness, a sense of humour and of course, the trademark moustache. The viewing public – the consumer of the 'Clark Gable' brand – demanded and got consistency of their brand.

The Hollywood system and its managers took the 'raw product' of actors and actresses, gave them new names, built their personalities, helped mould distinctive styles for them and through their films and massive public relations campaigns created 'stars'. They helped create a 'star mix' and then worked tirelessly to maintain it.

Norma Jean Baker was just another hopeful actress but under new management was to become one of Hollywood's most famous stars. With a new 'brand' name (Marilyn Monroe), a new personality (the not-so-dumb dumb-blonde), new 'all-white' packaging (from her hair to her underwear) and a PR campaign that was, at least, the equal of most modern day advertising campaigns Marilyn became, and remains, one of the true 'star brands' of Hollywood or indeed of the world.

The parallel is clear – the Hollywood stars had their managers to help them build and maintain their careers, so too do brands. Behind famous brands are their brand managers.

It was in the 1930s that the brand management system was first introduced by Procter & Gamble. They saw a brand manager's role as two-fold: to champion the brand and to come up with new ideas, new ways to beat the competition. Procter & Gamble referred to them as "the managing directors of their brands" but they equally could have been called brand agents.

An example that further demonstrates this parallel between brand managers and the stars' managers is Marlboro. Like Clark Gable, Marlboro needed to be re-launched before it became a success. Like Marilyn, its name was changed, albeit less drastically and, like both Clark Gable and Marilyn Monroe, it was given a new character and a new image.

Marlboro started life as 'Marlborough' and was positioned as a sophisticated cigarette targeted at women. Each cigarette had a distinctive red filter tip which led to the famous (infamous) advertising line "A cherry tip for your ruby lips". It wasn't a huge success.

It was re-launched in the 1950s, in a distinctive red and white flip top box losing the *'ugh'* along the way to become 'Marlboro'. It was now targeted at men and not surprisingly its character and image underwent a major overhaul. It became rugged and tough. It was given a new pioneering image. The advertising also changed, moving away from 'ruby lips' to the now famous Marlboro cowboy, the epitome of this new character.

It is a character and style that has brought the brand enormous success and which has been maintained ever since. The only exceptions are where advertising restrictions have forced Philip Morris, the brand's owner, to change the formula.

For example, in the UK, advertising regulations now exclude the use of any potentially healthy imagery in the promotion of cigarettes, new advertising has had to be developed without the cowboy. It conforms to the regulations but still remains true to the rugged, tough, American, pioneering character developed for the brand by its managers back in the 1950s.

More recently, Hugh Davidson in his excellent book *Offensive Marketing* defines a brand manager as:

> *The executive responsible for the overall marketing, and particularly promotion of a specific brand. Job function ranges from a co-ordination role to one in which profit objectives are built in.*

In reality there is rarely *one* individual responsible for the overall marketing of any one brand, indeed the actual title 'brand manager' is most often the title given to a fairly junior member of a much bigger brand management team. The real *manager* of a brand can be:

♦ *The brand manager*

A junior manager with two to five years experience. Typically with a marketing background, he or she is responsible for the day-to-day management of the brand.

♦ *The marketing manager*

A more senior manager with five to ten years experience who oversees the management of a range of products under one brand or a range of related brands.

♦ *The marketing director*

The senior executive charged with controlling the marketing of a company's brands, normally with 10 or more years experience. A marketing director is the person who takes the key decisions that will ultimately shape the brand's future and will traditionally have final responsibility for the brand's profitability.

♦ *The managing director*

An executive who has overall responsibility for the direction of the whole company but who often is the real brand manager particularly if his/her background is in marketing or if the company is dominated by one very powerful brand. Richard Branson is the real manager of the Virgin brand.

More often than not the brand's real managers or management are a combination of the above along with a supporting cast which includes the market research manager, design agency, advertising agency and media agency.

So it is perhaps not surprising that it is often said that brand managers (and even marketing managers) have '*no*' power which means literally they have the power to say 'no' but not to give the ultimate 'yes'. If they say 'yes' to a proposal, more often than not it merely moves up the hierarchy of the marketing department. It is the marketing director or managing director who has real power. It is these more senior executives who make all the really important decisions regarding a brand's management. They will finally agree a change in product formulation, a significant pack redesign or a major new advertising campaign.

Andrew Seth, a former managing director of Lever Brothers, went even further recently and said in his article "Brand New Days" (in *Marketing* 4 December 1997) that:

> *The role of a brand manager is not serious anymore. It has become a gofer role.*

It is true that the growth of global brands and centralised marketing departments has significantly reduced the 'local' brand managers' ability to change or even influence key elements of the brand he or she is supposed to be managing. The brand manager's role is nowadays more operational than it was 60 years ago. It often means simply implementing a strategy which has been developed and agreed centrally.

Whilst this means that any one brand manager may not be involved in all aspects of what is increasingly the bigger, more complex and more expensive task of managing a brand, it doesn't mean that brands aren't still managed. (For simplicity I will continue to use the term 'brand manager' and ask that that you, the reader, interpret them both in the broadest sense, i.e. the brand's management team.)

David Arnold, in his book, *The Brand Manager's Handbook*, contends that a brand manager:

> . . . *stands at the junction of company and customer and must integrate the totally different dynamics of two worlds.*

Brands are in many ways the public face of a company. They are its wares by which it is known. The brand's managers therefore have to manage both the internal workings of the company (production, sales, research and development, accounting) and meet its demands for sales, market share and profit whilst balancing these against the demands of the brand's consumers.

Therefore, unlike many other company disciplines, the brand's managers needs what Hugh Davidson calls a 'double perspective'. They must have an outward perspective on the needs and views of the brand's potential consumers whilst

The Brand Manager 's Double Perspective

THE CONSUMER COMPANY INTERFACE

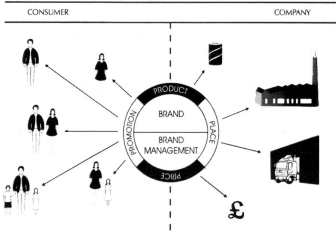

simultaneously maintaining an inward perspective on their company's resources and competencies. At its most basic, their job is to manage and match the two – profitably.

Another analogy sometimes used is that the brand manager is a juggler, managing the myriad of different and complex demands that descend on him from all sides. Good brand managers keep all the balls in the air, the best brand managers not only do that but move forward along a chosen path. By becoming Jacks-of-all-trades they become masters of one – brand management.

While a brand manager's specific roles and responsibilities are many and varied, they are often summarised as 'the four Ps': *product, price, place and promotion.*

Product   Put simply, the 'what?' of brand management. The brand manager oversees all aspects of the product from its size to its formulation. The naming of a brand or developing new products to be launched as part of that brand and other specific tasks. (See chapter six: How do brands get their names?) The role also includes any improvements to the product and its performance and the development and introduction of new flavours or varieties to meet the changing needs of the consumer.

The recent disastrous launch of 'new improved' Persil Power which, rather than delivering better results, damaged not only the clothes it was supposed to be cleaning but the brand's whole reputation demonstrates that while a brand is more than a product, a good product is a prerequisite for a successful brand. Managing that product is therefore vital to a brand's success.

Price   The brand manager develops and manages a pricing strategy for the brand, in other words 'how much?'. Is the brand a premium-priced offering with the likely implications of lower sales but higher profits, or is it a value-for-money brand with a lower price point but a high demand.

For many manufacturer brands the key issue of pricing strategy today is what is the brand's sustainable premium over the retailer branded equivalent product? The ability of a brand to maintain a higher premium over the long-run is a reflection of the strength of that brand.

Managing the brand's final price is, however difficult as more often than not the manufacturer/owner of the brand is not the retailer. In many cases nowadays it is a combination of retailer and brand owner that sets the final price. However, there a number of instances where the retailer, who obviously has final control, may decide to change the price. For example, they may want to use the brand as a special offer to draw new customers to their stores and so they reduce the price.

There are also exceptions where the brand and the retailer are linked – for example in petrol, with Shell or Esso, or other retail based brands like The Body Shop. Here the manufacturer obviously has control over the final price.

Place   The 'where?' of a brand, through what
                 channels is a brand distributed. Where is the
                 brand available? Is it delivered directly to your
                 door or does it go from manufacturer to retailer
                 to customer? If it is the latter there are many
                 types of retailers, which are important to the
                 brand in question?

                 In recent years drinks and confectionery
                 brands have found themselves more business
                 by finding or creating new sites where we,
                 their consumers, can buy them. Many DIY
                 stores now have sweets by their counters and
                 there has been a significant growth in vending
                 machines. You can find Coca-Cola vending
                 machines everywhere from car parks to school
                 halls. Place is a vital part of any brand's
                 strategy, if no-one knows where to find a
                 brand how can they buy it?

Promotion   The brand manager formulates and
                 implements a promotional plan, which
                 includes all the 'tools' for presenting the brand
                 to its potential consumers – advertising, public
                 relations and promotions. (The role of
                 advertising in encouraging consumers to buy
                 brands is discussed in detail in chapter ten.)

                 Promotions are the 'special offers' of the
                 branded world whether these are price
                 promotions (e.g. 10p off next purchase) or
                 loyalty promotions like collection-based
                 promotions (e.g. free mug for four proofs of
                 purchase). They include the strange sounding
                 BOGOF!, which put more politely means 'Buy
                 One Get One Free'.

                 Public relations or more grandly 'reputation
                 management' is the service provided by
                 specialist agencies to help present and manage
                 the perception of a brand with the media and
                 other key influencing groups up to and
                 including the government.

A number of observers contend that there is a fifth 'P'.

Some say it is *packaging*, 'the silent salesman' as it is sometimes called. However, packaging, whilst a vital part of a brand's make-up and appeal, is more often than not included as either part of the product itself or as part of the promotion of the brand. It is difficult to see how if one makes a case for packaging, a similar case for advertising could not be made and then the simplicity of this model, along with the alliteration, would disappear.

Others argue, more convincingly, that in the case of service brands there is often a fifth 'P': *people*. Service brands rely on the brand interacting with its consumer and often this means person to person contact. In cases like this a brand's people – its workforce – can be its greatest asset or its greatest weakness.

At Disneyland they say that the car park attendant can often be the most important person in their organisation. Why? Because they may be the first person a customer comes in contact with and if they are bright, happy and well-informed and can pass on a useful tip with a smile and a cheery word then the whole day for that customer can get off to a great start.

Product, Price, Place, Promotion, (People) – the four (five) Ps are a useful summary of what a brand manager does. In his sequel to *Offensive Marketing*, *Even more Offensive Marketing*, Hugh Davidson breaks down what brand managers do into more detail and examines how much time is spent on different types of activities. He states that:

> *In mature Marketing Departments, line marketing people frequently spend 80 to 90 per cent of their time on short-term tactical activity.*

He quotes client surveys by Oxford Corporate Consultants to suggest that this 80 per cent short-term activity or *'housekeeping'* includes sales promotion, routine advertising, routine market research, pricing, discounts, sales forecasting, range extension and monitoring results, while the remaining 20 per cent is spent on 'development' including strategy development, innovative market research, new product development, value improvement, channel strategy, relationship marketing and external communication.

Hugh Davidson's contention is that in many organisations line marketers or brand managers (in the broader sense) spend too much time on housekeeping and often fail to play a leading role in defining and developing the company's overall strategy. However, they actually spend their time, it would appear that the brand's managers are the power behind the throne and if they do their job properly then a brand can live on and on.

A final thought and perhaps a more cynical view of what brand managers really do is suggested by Graham Harding and Paul Walton in their lighthearted but informative *Bluff your way in Marketing*. They suggest three Rs as a more appropriate summary of most brand managers real-life actions:

Repackage   *Put the old brand in a smart new pack.*

Relaunch   *Trumpet the new pack, a new formulation or just a new advertising campaign.*

Resign   *Move on to the next, hopefully, higher-paid job before the results are known.*

This chapter began by drawing a parallel between the Hollywood star system and the brand management system. It suggested that both systems worked to create, and then manage, a 'mix' that would appeal to the public.

In the next few chapters, some of the elements of a brand mix. What brand's managers do and why, will be explored in more detail, beginning with brand naming.

6

How do brands get their names?

Would you call a brand of coffee *Bonka*? Would you call a lemonade *Pschitt*?

Perhaps surprisingly, both these brands *really* do exist.

Bonka comes from Spain where it is probably the first choice for that late night moment when your date asks whether you would like to come back for a . . . coffee.

Pschitt comes from France and whatever you may think, I am assured by

my French friends that it tastes delicious.

There are many other examples of brand names like these, brand names that don't travel well. Indeed Interbrand, an international company which specialises in helping firms develop brand and corporate names, has its own 'Black Museum' just for such names.

Other black museum exhibits include *Kack* (toffee from the continent) *Krapp* (toilet paper from Scandinavia) and *Bums* (biscuits from Sweden).

The Vauxhall Nova which sounds sensible enough is also included. In Spain, No-va is translated as 'does not go'.

So developing a new brand name isn't as easy as it might first appear. It is always important to consider what unfortunate associations your chosen name might have in other countries, particularly if one day you might want to sell it there.

Other guidelines for anyone or any company developing a new brand name would include the following:

1. *The name should be appropriate for the product or service.* An obvious example is Cadbury's Crunchie which is, not surprisingly, crunchy.

    Less obvious is Apple Computers, a name which at the time of its introduction, ran counter to the rest of the technologically led market. It was, however, entirely appropriate for a computer that wanted to be 'user-friendly' and aimed to demystify the whole market.

    As Apple themselves have said of their choice:

    > *The apple gives a positive feeling. It is non-threatening.*
    > *It has a healthy connotation – an apple a day keeps the*
    > *doctor away. It connotes a warm personal image.*

2. *It should be easy to pronounce or rather it should be able to pass the 'bar test'.* The bar test originates in the drinks market and is a check on the suitability of any new name. You simply imagine going up to a bar and asking for a. . .? Do you feel good or do you feel foolish?

    If the name sounds all right and you could imagine yourself using it, then the name passes. If, however, you think you might stumble over the name or not be able to pronounce it, then it fails and you need to find another name.

    Interestingly there are a few cases where over time the pronunciation of a brand name has changed. An example would be Nestlé which for years was pronounced 'nes-alls' but thanks to an awful lot of money and advertising is now increasingly known as 'nes-lay'. In fact, it's not only brand names that go through these name changes, certain foreign cities' names seem to change overnight on the news and Kim Bassinger, or rather Kim Base-inger, is similarly trying to overcome years of mispronunciation.

3. *It should be unique.* While this sounds easy enough you have to remember that there are now some 50 million registered trademarks around the world. Therefore it isn't surprising that on occasions some companies will now resort to buying names from other firms who have already registered the name they want.

4. *It should be suitable for use on packaging and in other promotional materials, including advertising.* Many if not most brand names are relatively short – six to nine letters long. This is not because their originators particularly like short names but because they realise that there is limited space on the product or its pack to put that name.

5. *It must take account of how, if at all, it will be used in connection with other brands.* Is it a house or product brand? Will it endorse or be endorsed by other brands? Will it stand alone as the only brand name on the pack?

   The answers to these questions obviously impact on the possibilities that can then be considered. As an unendorsed product brand there is no restriction but if the house brand is dominant or even just an endorsement then the relationship needs to be carefully considered.

To return to our Nestlé example, here the importance of the house brand is reflected in the chosen names for Nestlé's coffee range brand, Nescafé, and its tea brand, Nestea. It doesn't take a genius to suggest that if they were to launch a hot chocolate brand it might be called Neschoc. (Neschocolate being too long!)

These then are the 'rules' or guidelines for creating new brand names but how do brands get their names?

Like babies, most 'newborn' brands get their names from their 'parents' who in the case of brands are their creators or owners. There really was a Mr Cadbury, a Dr Kellogg and even a Mr Birdseye.

There was a Mr Marks and a Mr Spencer, a Mr Rolls and a Mr Royce, a Mr Tate and a Mr Lyle, but while there was a Mr Brooke, he never had a partner called Bond. Arthur Brooke just thought that together the two names *"seemed to sound well"*.

Mr Bond is not the only mysterious non-person in the history of brand naming. Personifying a brand by giving it a person's name and image is common practice on both sides of the Atlantic. In the UK, if truth be known, there is no Mr Kipling nor was there ever one, at least not one who made the *"exceedingly good cakes"*. He was invented by the advertising agency J Walter Thompson. In America there is a famous and very large brand of cooking and baking aids and mixes that bears the name 'Betty Crocker'. Wally Olins tells 'her' story:

> *Betty Crocker, that indomitable sprightly middle-western housewife, has been producing her homespun recipes for General Mills and its predecessors since 1921 or thereabouts. Betty Crocker not only writes recipes, she signs her name. She has had her portrait painted on several occasions (like Dorian Gray, she doesn't age) and she has appeared on radio programmes. And, of course, Betty doesn't really exist. She is made up, a figment of the imagination of all the people, within the company and its advertising agencies, who have worked on the Betty Crocker concept for most of this century.*

Betty was a creation. In fact, she was created as the by-product of a consumer offer. In 1921, a promotion for the Gold Medal flour brand, then owned by the Washburn Crosby Company, was run, whereby if a consumer correctly completed a jigsaw of a milling scene they were rewarded with a pincushion in the shape of a flour sack.

Along with their entries, thousands of people sent in questions about their baking problems. The advertising manager of the time, Sam Gale, believed that it would be more appropriate and believeable if the responses to those questions came from a woman and so Betty Crocker or at least her signature was invented.

In 1924 she acquired a voice and appeared on radio for the first time. In 1936 her portrait was painted for the first time. Since then Betty has been painted by a number of artists.

In 1941, by which time she was known to nine out of ten American housewives, she became a brand name on the product packaging. By 1945 she was known to nine out of ten American housewives and was the best known woman in the US next to Eleanor Roosevelt.

In 1961, the *Betty Crocker's New Picture Cookbook* offered its readers advice attuned to the times with entreaties: *"Think pleasant thoughts while working and a chore will become a labour of love."* The 1986 and 6th version, by contrast, helps its readers save time in the kitchen and produce lively meals.

The Betty Crocker brand name now covers more than 130 different products and in her latest guise Betty is not one woman but 75 women. For a recent campaign General Mills' advertising agency has taken photographs of 75 different Betty Crocker users and blended them together to create a new modern image for Betty. (See the colour section for all the portraits.)

If a brand isn't named after a person, real or imaginary, probably the next most likely source will be the brand itself – what it is, what it does or the values it represents. Many of the resulting brand names need little or no explanation. Take these three retail examples:

- Kwikfit is where you go to get tyres and brakes fitted quickly.
- The Co-op is indeed a co-operative society.
- Sainsbury's Homebase is not surprisingly Sainsbury's 'base' from where you can buy all manner of things for your 'home'.

There are, however, various 'games' that are played to add distinctiveness and originality to names. They include the *creative* spelling of part of all of the name, like the 'Kwik' in Kwikfit and Kwiksave or the chilled milkshake called Frijj. Then there are names that are obviously in need of a *fix*, that is a prefix or a suffix. These include, for example, the Vauxhall off-road, 4x4 car that allows you to travel out to the frontiers and beyond. It was christened the Front(i)er-a. Further ideas come from foreign languages, as this quotation from an Interbrand brand manager explains:

> *Latin is a common source of inspiration (for example, Aquascutum means 'weathershield', Volvo means 'I roll') so when Ford wanted a suitable name for their new world car, Mondeo sprang from the Latin word 'mondo' meaning 'guess what?'.*

Another favourite method for creating new brand names is the *'worger'* or 'word merger'. This is where two appropriate words are selected and then squashed together to create a completely new word. Hence in the 1980s, Hasbro's new game, in which players drew pictures of words to try and communicate their meaning, used 'picture' and 'dictionary' to create 'Pictionary'.

Worgers are used throughout the world, when Ole Kirk Christiansen invented a new toy, he merged two Danish words 'leg godt' which mean 'play well' to make Lego. An historical worger is the origin of Hovis which is derived from the latin 'hominis vis' – 'the strength of man'.

One final method that is used is the *'Sun* headline approach' to brand naming. It is an approach that is currently very much in vogue – 'I Can't Believe It's Not Butter' and 'Too Good To Be True' are just two British examples, while the Norwegian facial moisturisers 'Kiss My Face' show that the technique is truly international.

It's a simple game, you just imagine you are the editor of *The Sun* newspaper and that you're looking for a headline to sum up the new brand. Viewed like this brand names such as 'Wash'n'Go' and 'Utterly Butterly' are obvious choices. I'm now looking forward to the launch of a new extra hot chilli sauce called 'Phew, Wot a Scorcher!'.

There are many other instances where the brand's name has little or nothing to do with the actual 'product'. Kodak was a name invented by George Eastman, who produced and introduced the first Kodak camera in June 1888. As he himself explained, not only did he produced the name for himself, he wanted it to mean nothing:

> *I devised the name myself . . . I knew a trade name had to be short, vigorous, incapable of being misspelled to an extent that would destroy its identity and, in order to satisfy trademark laws it must mean nothing. The letter K had been a favourite with me – it seems a strong, incisive sort of letter. Therefore, the word I wanted had to start with a K. It became a question of trying out a great number of combinations of letters that made words, starting and ending with 'K'. The word Kodak was the result.*

George Eastman - a man with a fondness for the letter 'K'.

The origins of some brands' names are now lost in the mists of time and only the stories remain. One example is Oxo, those most British of stock cubes, which were in fact the invention of Baron Justus von Liebig, a German. While it is known that the Oxo name was first introduced in 1899 to replace the less appetizing Carnis Extractum Liebig, nobody really knows the real origin of the name.

Perhaps the most romantic story is that it was inadvertently christened by an illiterate South American docker. This is based on the fact that the beef stock used by Liebig was shipped in from South America where it was produced as a by-product in the preparation of corned beef. The story goes that the illiterate dockers needed to distinguish between the stock and the corned beef and that one enterprising soul started to mark up the crates with different symbols so that everyone could tell them apart. He marked the corned beef X-O-X and the stock O-X-O.

A lovely story that explains why Oxo is Oxo but doesn't explain why Fray Bentos Corned Beef isn't called Xox.

7

What is brand personality and why do brands need one?

If you were asked to choose a brand, any brand, and then to describe it, not as a product, but as if it was a person you'd probably think that it was a pretty strange request. However, once you had put that to one side, you might be surprised to find just how easily you could do it.

Take a brand and ask yourself, is it young or old? Is it male or female? Where does it come from? Is it an extrovert or an introvert? Would it be the life and soul of the party? Would it tell jokes? If so, what sort of jokes would it tell?

Let's take an example: The Volkswagen Beetle.

As a product the VW Beetle has been around for a while, yet its personality is very much 'young at heart'. It's male but definitely not macho. He is (on the assumption 'he' is male) German and he is outgoing. He has a happy, sunny character. He is, in fact, a bit quirky. He is reliable. He is a good friend.

A brand personality is all the human characteristics associated with a specific brand and the example above is therefore Volkswagen Beetle's brand personality.

Research has shown that our views of different brands' personalities are often highly consistent. When asked, we the consumers will often characterise a brand in very similar ways and indeed, if it is a strong brand, we can do so in great depth.

If, and where, differences do occur they are often for logical reasons. For example, it is not surprising that people who use a brand regularly often perceive that brand's personality much more clearly and more positively, whereas someone who uses a competitive brand may have less well-defined and more negative views about it.

For example a Citroën driver may believe his car with its unique hydraulic systems and distinctive styling to be modern, sophisticated, French and very stylish, while a non-user may well feel it is an idiosyncratic, unreliable, even strange brand. Cars are in fact a good example of the power of brand personality. If cars had no personalities would so many people give them nicknames?

So why is brand personality important?

In a world where the advance of technology means that it is now easier for one manufacturer to copy another one's product and to do so more quickly than ever before, brand personality is a key means of creating differentiation and maintaining a point of difference over a period of time.

We all meet thousands and thousands of other people in our lives and while there are physical differences between them, it is often their different personalities that help us see them as individuals, distinct in their own right. With products, where there are often less physical differences than between different people, personality can play an even bigger part in differentiating one from another.

In other words, two products can be very similar but if they have different personalities they can be two very distinct brands. Let us compare two brands of washing powders, Persil and Ariel. As products they are pretty similar and out of their packaging we might be hard pressed to tell them apart, yet they are very different brands because their personalities are very different.

Persil is like a caring, practical, sensible, down-to-earth Mum whereas Ariel is an efficient, effective, clean-cut, male scientist. As brands they are likely to appeal to different people whilst delivering broadly similar functional benefits.

Brand personality can therefore, not only help create differences between brands, it can help create appeal in brands. As Professor Leslie de Chernatory and Dr Francesca Dall'Olmo Riley say in their paper "*Branding in the Service Sector*":

> It (brand personality) is a powerful aspect of branding
> since there is evidence showing that when consumers
> choose between competing brands they do so according
> to the fit between the brand's personality and the
> personality they wish to project.

A Caring Mum?

An Efficient Scientist?

Earlier, in chapter three (Why do we buy brands?) it was argued that we buy brands, not just for what they do for us, but what they say about us to others and what they say to us about ourselves. A brand's personality is one of the key means by which a brand does this. We choose brands partly because they are a reflection of the sort of person we are or would like to be.

We use brands and their personalities as one way in which we can express ourselves. The purchase and use of brands can be akin to wearing a badge, "Oh yes he's a BMW driver". We want to be like the brand or aspire to its values. The purchase and use of a particular brand says something about who we are and who we would like to be, to ourselves and importantly to others.

Brands are a means of self-expression. The resurgence of Jeep with its rugged, outdoor, masculine personality and its off-the-road capabilities has become one way in which an increasing number of frustrated urban consumers have been able to express one aspect of their personality, or desired personality, even if their current lifestyle precludes them from living it for real.

Indeed, an increasing number of observers believe that as more and more of the traditional social and cultural barriers break down it will be our role as consumers that will define who we are. We will literally become what we eat, what we drink, what we wear, what we wash our hair with...

Interestingly we don't always choose brands that are exactly like ourselves and, in fact, we can happily choose brands that have personality traits that aren't particularly likeable in themselves. Instead they may just reflect a trait of a personality that is appropriate to our choice. (This notion of 'brandographics', defining a person by his use of brands, is a theme explored further in chapter seventeen.)

Paul Southgate in his book *Total Branding by Design* explains how this can be so:

> *A brand's personality is often **not** the same as that of its target market. Some brands do, in effect, hold a mirror to their consumers, saying 'buy me because I'm just like you'. Persil is arguably one such. But other brands project personalities which are quite different from their consumers. Ariel, for example, is bought mainly by women but has a decidedly masculine brand personality. It doesn't say 'buy me because I'm like you' but 'buy me because I'm a scientist and I know my subject so you can rely on me'.*

> *This brings me on to my second point. An appropriate brand personality is not necessarily one which consumers **like** (though this often helps). Sometimes it can be more important that consumers **respect** it. Or **trust** it. Sometimes, a brand can even make a virtue out of personality traits which are not in themselves particularly likeable. Remy Martin, for example, is an out-and-out snob. BMW conforms to the teutonic stereotype of being utterly devoid of humour. Marks & Spencer is a middle-class male of the most pernickety variety. Yet these traits of brand personality not only fail to put us off buying that cognac, that car, those shirts – they are in each case part of the brand's appeal.*

Hence, in the case of Ariel, the role of a brand personality is not so much a means of self-expression for the consumer but rather it is a representation of the brand's functional attributes. This representation is another means through which the creation of brand personality can add to a brand's appeal. An appropriate personality can bring to life the functional benefits a brand is offering us.

Probably the most powerful way in which this is achieved is through the use of a visual symbol or image, a brand icon, that captures the essence of the personality and conveys it succinctly. (These brand icons are explored in more detail in chapter eight.) However, a brand icon is not the only method by which a brand's personality is created or evolves. A brand's personality is connected to nearly everything linked with that brand.

The product category that a brand is in, can immediately set up expectations and start to define its personality. Sports cars like Lotus, Ferrari and Porsche are generally all thought to be racy and sexy, whilst banks like National Westminster and Lloyds reflect the stereotypical image of bankers, namely older, professional, serious men. A brand name like Jaguar is chosen specifically because it encapsulates the desired brand personality.

Specific product features that a brand has can be a powerful driver of its personality. As we have seen, BMW and Volkswagen are both known to come from Germany and hence are imbued with some of the characteristics that are generally attributed to Germans.

Provenance is in fact one of the product features that is often most exploited by brand owners to help create a brand's personality. Taking just the lager market, Fosters and Castlemaine use their Australian origins and its associated characteristics, Carlsberg plays off its Danish origins, Lowenbrau and Becks are German and proud of it, Kronenborg is French. Stella Artois on the other hand is Belgian and, perhaps because of that country's lack of stereotypical personality traits, derives its personality from sources other than its place of origin.

In fact in the UK much of Stella Artois' personality is derived from two other product features: its price and its heritage. These features are tellingly communicated for Stella via its advertising which uses the idea that the brand is *reassuringly expensive*. Advertising is one of the other most powerful means of creating a brand personality and this (and advertising's other roles) are explored more fully in chapter ten.

David A Aaker in his book, *Building Strong Brands* compiles a whole list of brand personality drivers. In addition to those already mentioned he notes that user imagery either actual or perceived, sponsorship, a brand's CEO (as in the case Virgin's Richard Branson or Microsoft's Bill Gates), the packaging and celebrity endorsements can all be important factors in creating a personality for a brand.

Indeed perhaps the best way to sum up how brand personality is created is to recognise that when it comes to branding, everything communicates.

8

What are brand icons and what roles do they play?

Throughout the world the golden arches of McDonald's are instantly recognisable, but why is the 'M' drawn with those distinctive arches and what do they represent?

Thomas Hine in his book *The Total Package* tells the story of how Louis Cheskin, a designer, worked with McDonald's at the time when they were considering abandoning arches as an architectural feature for the outlets. While agreeing that it might be sensible to move away from arches in the buildings:

> *[Cheskin] advised that the memory of the arches be kept in the form of the M in 'McDonald's'. His case was based, he said, on research that showed that "the arches had Freudian applications to the subconscious mind of the consumer and were great assets in marketing McDonald's food". In other words, Cheskin said, the arches are "mother McDonald's breasts, a useful association if you're replacing home-made food".*

Whether or not the arches do subconsciously remind us of our mother's breasts may be open to question, but what they undoubtedly do is demonstrate the fact that marketing is a visual business. How brands look, how they present themselves is a crucial part of their make-up. As the old, but often true, saying goes, *'a picture is worth a thousand words'*.

Visual aspects of a brand include the packaging, the advertising and the way in which the brand name itself is depicted. They all play their part in building the image of the brand in our minds. It's hard to think of Coca-Cola and not think of the flowing, white, copperplate script on the bright red background or the distinctively curvaceous bottle. The bottle is known as both the *Mae West* bottle, because of that shape and the *Christmas* bottle because the shape itself was patented originally on 16 November 1915 and then again on 25 December 1923.

This book doesn't aim to explore packaging, logo or corporate design in any great depth. I am not a designer and there are many good books on those subjects already. However, as discussed in the previous chapter, a brand icon – the symbols, signs or characters that become intrinsically linked with a brand – are a key means by which brand personality can be expressed directly or indirectly. This chapter will explore them in more detail.

Below are a series of famous brand icons, all of which happen to be animals. See if you can name the brand associated with each.

They are of course, Camel's camel, World-Wide Fund For Nature's panda and the Playboy bunny. These three examples also represent the three main types of brand icon which are:

(a) an icon depicting the brand's name itself;

(b) an icon depicting an element of what the product is or does;

(c) an icon depicting the character or personality of the brand.

The latter two types are therefore expressions of the brand's personality, either directly as in the third group or indirectly through the depiction of the brand's functionality.

The first type need not be an expression of a brand's personality as it may merely visualise a brand name and that need not relate to the brand's personality.

For example, and returning to the animal theme, there is Penguin books. Nobody seems to know exactly why Penguin books are called Penguin. One story goes that it was the secretary of Allen Lane, Penguin's founder, who made the original suggestion for the name. Allen Lane was supposedly delighted with this idea and dispatched Edward Young, a 21 year-old office boy to London Zoo to do some sketches. His original icon was replaced fifteen years later with the design we know today.

Camel's camel is also based on a drawing, but rather than a sketch by an office boy the drawing in question was done by the founder of the R J Reynold's company himself. It depicts 'Old Joe' – a real life camel who featured in the Barnum & Bailey circus of 1913. 'Old Joe' has since been used on the pack, in advertising and in point of sale material. He is quite possibly the world's most famous camel but why the brand is called Camel in the first place I simply don't know.

The story of the red roofed Pizza Hut icon is another example of this category but not quite as you might expect. While it depicts the hut in the name, it wasn't only the original restaurant's appearance that led to the name and then the icon. Per Mollerup tells the story in his excellent book, *Marks of Excellence*:

Pizza Hut, the fast food chain, did not derive its name entirely from its original premises. Things happened the other way around. When the restaurant first opened in Wichita, Kansas, in 1958, there was only space for nine characters on the existing sign. The founding Carney brothers wanted the word 'Pizza' to be part of the name, but there were only three letters left. Since the house looked like a hut, the name became Pizza Hut. The characteristic roof, now part of the trademark was not added until 1969.

In the second category, where the icon depicts some element of what the brand is or does, there are also lots of examples, some of which are old, some pretty new.

BMW's blue and white symbol reflects the brand's origins as an aircraft manufacturer at the time of the First World War. The circle divided into four quarters, alternately coloured blue and white, originally had nothing to do with cars. It was in fact a graphic depiction of a whirling propeller.

On the other hand Cadbury Dairy Milk's 'glass and a half' icon is a more recent invention. It was created as an effective graphic depiction of the milk that actually goes into making Cadbury's Dairy Milk. There is a glass and a half of full cream milk in every half pound.

It's a powerful symbol that helps reinforce Cadbury's credentials as a manufacturer of the highest quality dairy milk chocolate and supports their claim to be *"**The** Chocolate,' **The** Taste"*. In fact, Cadbury claim that the amount of milk used in one year's production of Dairy Milk Chocolate would fill nearly 14½ Olympic size swimming pools.

Within this category there are a number of icons which are literally made of the brand. Bibendum – the Michelin Man is perhaps the most famous. Marjorie Stiling tells the story of his birth in her book *Famous Brand Names, Emblems and Trademarks*:

> *At the Lyons Exhibition in 1898, brothers André and Edouard Michelin, inventors of these tyres, found their stand manager had stacked the tyres in assorted sizes in order to try and present them in a novel way. "Look André," said Edouard, pointing to one of the stacks of tyres, "if it had arms it would look like a man."*
>
> *André recalled this incident when, some while later, he was visited by a Monsieur O'Galop and shown some sketches for advertisements. André caught sight of a cartoon which O'Galop had just received from a German beer manufacturer. It portrayed a rotund gentleman raising his beer mug and announcing 'Nunc est Bibendum' – 'Now is the time to drink'. André told O'Galop of Edouard's imaginative observation at the exhibition and the artist got to work. The tyre man replaced the beer drinker.*

Another example is Bertie Bassett, the man made out of Bassett's Liquorice Allsorts. Many believe that the inspiration for Bertie was none other than Bibendum himself.

WWF's panda was designed by Sir Peter Scott, the ornithologist, artist and founder of The World-Wide Fund For Nature. Of his design he is quoted as saying:

> *We wanted an animal that is beautiful, is endangered and one loved by many people in the world for its appealing qualities. We also wanted an animal that had impact with black and white printing to save money on printing costs.*

His design has delivered all that and more. Indeed as the charity changed its name from the 'World Wildlife Fund' to 'World-Wide Fund For Nature' it is highly likely that more people can recognise the logo than can correctly recall the brand's name.

A variation within this category is where the element of what the brand is or does is depicted metaphorically rather than literally. Legal & General's umbrella would be a good example. Its bright, multicoloured umbrella is eye-catching but, just as importantly, it is a good symbol for protection. Another example would be Fairy Liquid's baby. It is a metaphor for the product's softness and mildness.

Mythology is another source of inspiration within this category. Mercury is widely known as the messenger to the Roman gods. Less well known is the fact that he was a god himself. He was the god of roads and boundaries as well as being the god of commerce, trickery and theft.

Therefore it is perhaps not surprising that he has been used by a number of brands as an icon representing some aspect of themselves. He is seen holding a bunch of flowers and speeding on his way to deliver them in the Interflora icon. His winged foot was chosen by the founder of Goodyear, Frank A Seiberling to be that brand's icon.

Jaguar and its leaping cat is another interesting example because it is both an icon depicting the brand name and, because that name was chosen to reflect the brand's characteristics, it depicts those as well. The name Jaguar was chosen by the brand's founder, Sir William Lyons, because of associations with its grace, speed, power and beauty. The leaping cat icon depicts all this and embellishes it with style and sophistication.

As discussed earlier in this book, Marlboro was originally launched in the 1920s and then re-launched in 1955. The re-launch included what is now one of the world's most famous icons, the Marlboro Cowboy. The tough, lean, weather-beaten cowboy in the rugged Marlboro Country landscape was chosen because it encapsulated Philip Morris' desired personality for the re-launched brand – strong, independent, masculine and pioneering. It is a classic example of the third type of icon, one which is a depiction of the brand's character or personality.

The Marlboro Cowboy has been proven to be an inspired choice. It has become a very powerful and memorable icon. It (he) has travelled right round the globe and helped establish Marlboro as the world's leading international cigarette.

Another very masculine brand chose a somewhat softer icon for itself – a bunny. Admittedly they did not choose a soft, cuddly, toy bunny but a more sophisticated, man-about-town one, sporting a distinctive bow tie. The Playboy bunny, is another good example of an icon that reflects the brand's desired character and personality. As Per Mollerup says:

> *It (the bunny) serves as a metaphor to remind the Playboy reader of the magazine's uninhibited interest in sexuality. The bow tie and attentive ears suggest that the rabbit is both elegant and alert.*

In describing the different types of brand icons, many of the reasons why they were created have already been mentioned or at least alluded to. However, to summarise, what they are is a visual shorthand for the brand itself which, if successful, allows the brand to convey a great deal of information and meaning instantly in a form that can be both very appealing and highly memorable.

The Mercedes icon, a simple circle divided into three equal parts has come to stand for style, sophistication, high quality, German engineering and a real feeling of prestige. In the blink of an eye, the time it takes to recognise the icon, all that can be communicated. It's far quicker than speech, far quicker than reading.

Humans are a very visual species and hence colour, shape and form combined as images and icons are powerful tools

in the marketing of brands. The psychologist, Albert Mehrabian, examined people's perceptions of other people and concluded that:

> *55 per cent of the impression we make on others is determined by what they see. . .38 per cent is determined by what they hear and the remaining 7 per cent by the words we use.*

Whilst these icons are not people, they often are expressions of the brands' personalities and it is precisely because icons are visual that they facilitate this all important injection of personality. The style of an icon, what it is and how it is rendered communicates a great deal. To paraphrase a Bananarama song *"it ain't **just** what you say **but the** way that you say it, that's what gets results"*. Only in this case it's draw, not say. A good icon can have much more depth of meaning than the most carefully chosen word.

As discussed in earlier chapters, brands are much more than the sum of their physical parts. They appeal to both our heads and our hearts. It is the very fact that they have their own values and personalities that helps to give them their appeal and helps create the differences between them. Thus brand icons, which are a key means of expressing those values and personalities, are a vital part of the brand manager's armoury.

Other advantages of an icon are that it is often more visually appealing and potentially more memorable than a written word or words. As discussed earlier, Sir Peter Scott's panda is an admirable proof of this point. Visual icons by definition don't need words. This can also be a huge advantage where the brand in question needs to be able to travel across different countries with different languages or indeed to countries where literacy rates are low.

Nike's 'swoosh' is a perfect example. It is now as instantly recognisable in the backstreets of São Paolo, as it is in the backstreets of Scunthorpe.

However, perhaps the ultimate story of brand icons is the story of Guinness and the Irish State. In 1862 Guinness chose the O'Neill harp as its brand icon. Over the years the exact form changed (the number of strings has been reduced) but Guinness has continued to use the symbol in almost everything it does.

In 1922 when Ireland was declared an independent state, it decided that it also wanted to use the O'Neill Harp as its official symbol. Guinness didn't want to give up their icon. The situation was only resolved when the Irish State agreed to use a reversed image of the harp and therefore avoid any copyright problems. In the light of this it is not surprising that Guinness and Irishness are so closely linked.

9

What is brand positioning and where does it fit into the marketing mix?

A l Ries and Jack Trout offered the following definition in their famous book *Positioning: the battle for your mind* and whilst they talk about a company in this quotation, the definition holds for a brand.

> To succeed in our over-communicated society, a company must create a position in the prospect's mind, a position that takes into consideration not only a company's own strengths and weaknesses, but those of its competitors as well.

If a brand's values and personality are a summation and a reflection of its physical and its psychological attributes then brand positioning is how a brand is located in its marketplace and placed relative to its competitors. It is what a brand offers the target consumer and what differentiates that offer from the competition.

There are, therefore, four key elements to any brand positioning.

1. The target consumer.

2. The market in which the brand competes.

3. The offer it makes.

4. The elements that make that offer unique.

Ries' and Trout's 'prospects' or the target consumers are the first element. They are the people at whom the brand is aimed. The people who will buy or use the brand in question. They can be defined in a variety of ways, and more or less tightly, depending on the brand. For example Hedex may see its target consumers as anyone who gets a headache while Aller-Eze targets only those people who suffer from hayfever.

Target audiences can be defined by age, for example (and continuing the over-the-counter medicines theme) Calpol is targeted at children. However, it is possible to target by social class, sex, location or attitude. This latter category is known as psychographics. It defines and segments people based on their attitudes, so it is possible for a brand to consider targeting people who are 'young at heart' or who 'like to try new things'. In fact it is possible to target people who are users of specific brands, a theme which is explored in chapter seventeen on brandographics.

Secondly, what is the consumer's frame of reference? How do they perceive the brand and in which market is it competing? Now it may seem a remarkably easy exercise, to define what market you are in. However the failure to look beyond the obvious can cause long term problems for brands.

The marketing guru, Theodore Levitt, analysed the decline and fall of the great American railroads and argued that they suffered from a severe case of *'marketing myopia'*. They believed that they competed in the railroads business. They therefore failed to take account of new non-railroad competition – the motor industry – that went on to steal their customers and much of their market away. They would have perhaps developed a different strategy had they thought about the fact that they competed in the transportation business, not just the railroad business.

Monopoly is undoubtedly a board game and so competes with other board games, but it also competes in a broader leisure market with computer games, television and even playing sports. Defining the correct consumer reference for your brand is therefore important because it helps the brand's management team understand what needs their brand addresses and who are their real competition.

The third key element of any brand positioning, as already suggested, is what are the needs addressed by the brand? What does the brand do? What does it offer its target consumer?

Which leads directly onto the fourth and final element, how is this brand's offer differentiated against the competition. What

M

A R

K E T

I N G M

Y O P I A

A short-sighted approach to defining the market in which the brand competes.

makes the brand unique? What makes its offer special? We have already seen that in the case of brands, rather than just products, this can be a complex set of functional and emotional attributes.

However, perhaps the ultimate offer a brand can make is to simply claim it is the best in the world and that no-one does it better in its particular market. For example, British Airways positions itself as *'the world's favourite airline'*; in the shaving market, Wilkinson Sword claims to be *'the name on the world's finest blades'*.

Gillette which competes directly with Wilkinson Sword in the razor blades market has a positioning that at first could appear to be very close if not identical to that of Wilkinson Sword.

However, the two brands adopt a very different frame of reference. Wilkinson Sword positions itself in the 'blades' or shaving market while Gillette sees itself in the broader 'men's toiletries' market and so confidently and distinctively claims to be *'the best a man can get'*. Gillette backs this up with a wider range of products including after-shaves and deodorants.

For years, Harveys Bristol Cream has positioned itself as *'the best sherry in the world'*. More recently and following the transition of a number of its competitors into clearing banks, the Nationwide Building Society has repositioned itself as *'The World's No 1 Building Society'*.

So whilst being number one has obvious attractions, can being number two be positioned to a brand's advantage?

Avis has long been in that position in the car rental market behind the brand leader Hertz. How did they position this to their advantage? Well, they simply and honestly admitted the truth but then cleverly suggested that they were working flat out to change the situation.

> *Avis is only number two in rent-a-cars, so why go with us? We try harder.*

It was a brilliant piece of positioning. It not only suggested that Avis had the hunger and drive of a company that really wanted your business, but simultaneously hinted that Hertz might just be resting on its laurels and not doing as much as it could to retain your business. However, not all brands are as clever as they are honest. Iberia's positioning of itself as the fourth largest airline in Europe isn't compelling.

Brand positioning is normally long term but that does not mean that it has to be permanent. It is quite possible to reposition your brand. (Indeed Marlboro, as discussed in chapter five, is a classic example.)

A more recent example is the Quaker breakfast cereal brand, Sugar Puffs. From targeting a young-child audience they have repositioned themselves against an older child, early teenage target audience. This has been reflected in their advertising. Their famous brand icon, the honey monster, is still featured but instead of being an overgrown and somewhat clumsy teddy bear who pleaded *"Tell them about the honey, Mummy"*, he is now a much trendier character performing with pop groups and footballers.

Perhaps one of the most famous UK examples of a brand repositioning is Lucozade.

Lucozade was invented by a Newcastle chemist and was originally sold only through chemists as a semi-medicinal product. Its high level of glucose provided energy in an easy-to-digest and pleasant form for people who were feeling unwell and were unable, or unwilling, to eat.

Over the years it built a strong position in the market on the back of a proposition that it aided recovery. However, due partly to increasingly tough restrictions on the advertising claims it could make and more importantly the desire to grow the brand further, it was decided to try and broaden the brand's appeal by targeting not just the sick but the tired as well.

The obvious rationale being that while people are only ill some of the time they get tired much more frequently. Lucozade therefore was to become the glucose drink that *"helps you through the ups and downs of the day"*. Its core target group of users shifting from the sick to hard-working housewives. While this was a more mainstream positioning it was also one which didn't have the powerful appeal to a real consumer need in the way the original proposition had.

Hence in the early 1980s the positioning of the brand was reviewed again. Again it was decided that targeting the ill was too narrow an audience and it was decided to try to appeal to a much broader and growing group – the increasingly health conscious and very active, younger generation. Lucozade also wanted a positioning that would encourage the brand to be drunk regularly, not just on particular occasions such as when you are ill.

In 1983, with the help of the Olympic decathlete Daley Thompson, Lucozade launched its new positioning. It remained true to its original product form, the sparkling glucose drink, and true to its long standing core consumer offer of 'energy'. What it did was to pivot its positioning around this core proposition and reposition itself against a target audience that was the direct opposite of its original consumers.

Lucozade went from being the glucose drink that replaces lost energy for sick or tired people to being the great tasting drink that's full of energy for healthy and active people. Only now the benefit was not just energy it was '*110% NRG*'!

From advertising that featured sick children and hard-working mums through the Daley Thompson era, Lucozade has transformed its approach and has now featured snowboarding teenagers and loud rocking sound tracks. The new positioning has also been reflected in other elements of the marketing mix. The brand's graphic identity has been redesigned to make it more youthful and dynamic. Single serve bottle and cans have been introduced as packaging formats which are more appropriate to the new target audience than the original large glass bottles. The brand has also been extended in Lucozade Sports drinks and energy tablets.

It has proven to be a radical and highly successful repositioning of an old brand and clearly demonstrates the role brand positioning can have in perceptions and performance of a brand.

Another even more recent repositioning of a brand which, while less radical, has been more controversial, is that of the AA. The Automobile Association recently transformed itself from being the country's leading breakdown recovery service to *'the fourth emergency service'*. It now powerfully positions itself alongside the police, fire brigade and the ambulance service rather than mundanely referencing other breakdown services. Its whole corporate identity from logo to vans to handbooks, as well as its advertising, has been revamped to reflect this bold, new positioning. (An example of their advertising is included in the colour section.)

However, for some, the AA is claiming a position that has traditionally been owned by the coastguard service. Indeed, immediately after the relaunch there was some adverse publicity in the national press. This quickly died down and now it is the AA that owns 'the fourth emergency service' positioning in the mind of the consumer. Furthermore, in the marketplace, in terms of membership the repositioning has proven to have been very successful.

As we have seen throughout this book, when it comes to brands and branding, it is people's perceptions that really count and as Ries and Trout say:

> *Positioning is an organised system for finding a window in the mind.*

As discussed, positioning is a system based on four elements so, if you feel inclined to review a brand's positioning, or to try your hand at repositioning an existing brand, simply fill in the gaps in the format below:

For.................................(target consumer) ....

X is the ....(frame of reference) ....

that......................(needs the brand addresses)......................

with....(differentiating functional and emotional attributes)....

10

Why do brands advertise?

Strangely enough, one of the most famous names in advertising, Bill Bernbach, the founder of the international advertising agency Doyle Dane Bernbach, once said that advertising kills products. Well actually what he said was:

> *The fastest way to kill a **bad** product is **good** advertising.*

And this, rather than damning advertising, is in fact a backhanded compliment to its effectiveness.

What Bill Bernbach was arguing was that if the brand (product) is a poor one and fails to meet the needs of its customers then good advertising, which encourages lots of people to go out and buy the brand, will merely result in them finding out more quickly that the brand is no good. Consequently they will be highly unlikely to buy that particular brand again and it will soon die.

However, as most brands are of a good standard and actually do satisfy consumers needs, they will choose to use advertising for the most obvious reason. They want to sell more of their product. They want their brand to grow.

At its most basic, brands advertise because advertising encourages people to buy them. Indeed, Commodore James Thompson, the founder of another famous advertising agency, J Walter Thompson said in 1906:

> *Advertising copy is good when it achieves the effect intended, when it brings in trade. There is no other standard of value, outside of the ranks of theorists.*

While there is an undeniable logic to this, it is perhaps an over-simplification. Not all advertising is expected to create *instantaneous* sales, for example, the role of advertising in creating brand personality has already been discussed in chapter seven.

What's more, as the good Commodore suggests, there are numerous theorists who would, and do, consider that there are alternative advertising objectives of value. Philip Kotler, while agreeing with the central premise of the Commodore's argument, looks deeper into the process of advertising and explores the route we, the consumers, take to get to the actual decision to act. He suggests:

> *The ultimate response (of brand advertising), of course, is purchase and satisfaction. But purchase behaviour is the end result of a long process of consumer decision making. The marketing communicator needs to know how to move the target audience to higher states of readiness to buy.*
>
> *The marketer can be seeking a cognitive, affective or behavioural response from the target audience. That is, the marketer might want to put something into the consumer's mind, change the consumer's mind or get the consumer to act. Even here, there are different models of consumer response stages.*

In other words, Kotler is suggesting that the objectives of advertising need not necessarily be *directly* to get the consumer to buy a specific brand. There may be other objectives that are more indirect. The aim of the advertising might be to create awareness of a brand ("to put something into the consumer's mind") or to get the consumer to consider or re-consider something about the brand ("change the consumer's mind") and the reason why advertisers do this is to move the consumer through the different stages of a "decision-making process".

There are a number of different theories about the consumer decision-making process, which is the process by which we the consumer are moved along the path from blissful ignorance of a brand's existence to finally purchasing that brand. Kotler in his book *Managing Markets*, describes four slightly different models of a consumer "decision-making process".

Perhaps the most famous of these is the 'AIDA' model which was originally developed by E K Strong in his *Psychology of Selling* in 1925.

THE AIDA MODEL

Stages	AIDA
Cognitive ◆ gaining recognition	Attention
Affective ◆ affecting perceptions	Interest Desire
Behavioural ◆ affecting behaviour	Action

The model is based on the idea that the consumer goes through a logical sequence of stages before acting – buying a brand.

Attention   Firstly the consumer's attention must be gained. The consumer must be made aware of a brand.

Interest   Then the consumer must be encouraged to become interested in the brand.

Desire   Thirdly the consumer needs to be persuaded that the brand is desirable.

Action   Finally the consumer is encouraged to act on his desire and go out and buy the brand.

If this is the case then a brand and its advertisers need to design advertising that can either grab the attention, or hold interest, or try to create desire or call the consumer to action. It can try to do all of that but it is more likely that different ads will have different objectives.

In his well-known book *Defining Advertising Goals for Measured Advertising Results* (better known as DAGMAR), Colley lists 52 different advertising objectives. These, in turn, are often divided into three categories – informative, persuasive and reminder advertising. Some examples of these different types of objectives and resulting advertising executions are outlined below.

Informative

♦ To announce the launch of a new brand.

♦ To make people aware of existing services or attributes of a brand.

♦ To demonstrate how a brand works/what it does.

♦ To announce a product improvement.

Persuasive

♦ To build brand preference.

♦ To demonstrate that one particular brand is better than another/all others. (This is a sub-category in its own right, known as comparative advertising.)

♦ To change people's perceptions of a brand and its attributes.

♦ To persuade people to buy a brand now.

Reminder

♦ Maintaining a brand top-of-mind awareness.

♦ To remind people that they might/will need the brand in the near future.

♦ To remind people where they can get a brand.

♦ To assure people they have made a good choice of brand. (This is known as re-enforcement advertising and often used in car advertising as part of a long term aim to ensure re-purchase.)

All of this in many ways is still based on the notion that we move through a logical decision-making sequence and that advertising informs, then persuades and ultimately sells to us.

What this ignores or at least undervalues is the role of advertising in building and maintaining a brand and its values.

If a brand is, as previously argued, much more than the sum of its physical parts and its true strength lies in the mind, then it is important to recognise that advertising has traditionally been a powerful means of establishing and building those values in our minds. As we have seen, advertising is one of the ways in which brand personality is created, which in turn can be one of the reasons why we choose to buy a brand.

Oxo wouldn't be Oxo had it not been for the long running 'Katie' and 'Family' advertising campaigns. And while the ultimate aim of this advertising was undoubtedly to create sales, these sales are the sales of Oxo the brand, and that brand had to be built, developed, adapted and maintained over the years.

Oxo's advertising has been fundamental to its success. The advertising has helped build the emotional heart of the brand as well as communicate its functional benefits. The

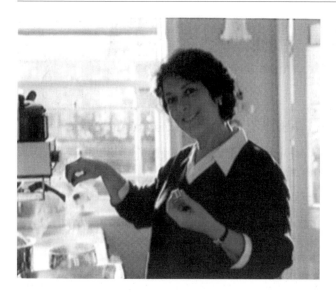

advertising has helped create the unique Oxo personality. Oxo is all about caring, warmth and the family. Oxo is much more than the little red cube. It has been described as:

> *A giant red casserole sitting on the kitchen table. When the lid is removed it draws the family to it like a magnet.*

So it can be argued that one reason why brands advertise is that advertising helps build brands out of products and this, in turn, is one of the reasons why we, the consumer, are more likely to buy them. All well and good in theory but still the vast majority of us claim that advertising doesn't affect our behaviour. We aren't swayed by the 'hidden persuaders'.

Well in practice there is actually an awful lot of evidence that we may be fooling ourselves and that at least some advertising does work and helps encourage us to buy a brand.

Take the lager market as just one example. It's hard to think of Heineken without thinking of its "*refreshes the parts other beers cannot reach*" campaign. Think of Carlsberg and you'll remember another famous advertising campaign... *probably*. Castlemaine certainly does give a XXXX about its advertising.

Every two years the Institute of Practitioners in Advertising runs an advertising effectiveness awards scheme. Advertising agencies and their clients, the brand owners, are invited to submit papers that demonstrate how well their advertising has worked. The most convincing papers win prizes and are subsequently published in the '*Advertising Works*' series of books.

Reviewing the list of past winners is like a roll-call of famous brands. It includes Andrex, BMW, Levi, Oxo, TSB and Castlemaine XXXX. The case histories don't claim that advertising was the only reason that a brand was successful, rather they aim to highlight and then measure the advertising's contribution.

Obviously each case is different and so naturally are the actual results but it is not surprising to see increased sales of 50 per cent, 100 per cent, 200 per cent or more! So while we may claim our behaviour isn't influenced by advertising, it seems that our actions speak louder than our words.

Let us take a final, more recent, example. It hasn't won an advertising effectiveness award yet but may well be a future contender. It is the case of the face-slapping orange genie and suggests not only have we '*been Tango'd*', but we have enjoyed it as well.

Tango is a fizzy, orange drink brand owned by Britvic. It competes with other sweet, fizzy, orange drinks like Sunkist and Fanta. However in the UK, the sweet, fizzy drinks market is dominated, like many others in the world, by Coca-Cola and fizzy orange was, until recently, a smaller, less exciting sector of the market. Tango's performance was steady if not spectacular, selling something like one million cans a year.

It, like most other fizzy drinks brands, was a regular advertiser on television but remained a relatively minor player in the market. Then in 1991, Tango appointed a new advertising agency – HHCL+Partners – a young, so called 'hot shop' creative agency. They were to develop a new advertising campaign based on the premise that: "*Nothing else gives you the hit of real oranges quite like Tango.*"

The ad they created featured an ordinary man in the street drinking a can of Tango, a spoof football commentary-style voice over and a small, fat man painted completely orange who was to slap our 'hero' around the cheeks. (See the colour plate section.) It was a literal dramatisation of Tango's Orange-iness.

Now, when the ad first appeared on television in January

1992, nothing else in the marketing mix had changed.

♦ The product hadn't been changed. It was the same old Tango – Tango had always been made with real oranges.

♦ It was in the same can, the same size with the same design it had used for a number of years. (However, the design was soon to change, moving to a new look that reflected the brand's new persona.)

♦ The price hadn't changed. It wasn't suddenly dropped or raised.

However, sales of Tango shot up – after one month sales were up over a quarter on the same period in the previous year!

People up and down the country loved the advertising. They liked its quirky humour, they liked its irreverence. It made people think about Tango either for the first time or in a new light. It didn't just make them think about it, it made them go out and buy the brand. One year after the launch of the campaign, sales were up 26 per cent year on year.

Tango have since built on that success. There have been new ads, new pack designs and new flavours, including Apple, Blackcurrant and Lemon. Tango is now undoubtedly a major force in the British fizzy drinks market and while it's not all due to the advertising it's certainly true that the brand has benefited from being "*Tango'd*"!

In more recent years an increasing number of people have contested the traditional theoretical models, stating they were too simplistic and that they are out of touch with today's consumer and therefore out of date. They argue that fundamental changes have taken place in society and that, while advertising will continue to be important for building and maintaining brands, it will play a less central role.

Perhaps one of the most vociferous of these challengers has been none other than HHCL+Partners, the creators of the Tango campaign. Established in 1986, their challenging views have caused much controversy in the industry and they have been called the *enfants terribles* of advertising.

In their manifesto "*Marketing at a Point of Change*" Adam Lury, one of the agency's founding partners, writes:

In the good old days, we all knew our place. What consumers did best was consume. Mass production led to mass consumption, identical units consumed by identical households. We (advertising agencies and brand managers) leaned on the certainty of numbers and the authority and credibility of science.

Behaviour was monitored and calculated. Text book acronyms like AIDA (attention, interest, desire, action) reduced human decision-making to the status of laboratory rat-hood.

Now the animals have taken over the farm, consumers have become customers.

No longer chips off the old C1C2 (a socio-economical classification of consumers) block, they are individuals who are more demanding, people who expect product/ service quality and who want information about what they are buying.

Forty years of commercial television means that they are smarter; not only are they media literate they are 'market literate'. Marketing is no longer a mystery. They watch and they learn. They know about product life-cycles, product similarity, pricing strategy – "You're buying a lot of off-peak airtime," a 24-year-old observes in a focus group discussion.

In the language of transactional analysis the roles have shifted. Customers are no longer prepared to be the 'child', ever credulous, submissive to authority, following the agenda set by the parent or adult. They have grown up, they want to be treated as equals in any transaction, adult to adult.

They want to be involved in the process and increasingly they want recognition that it is their agenda that is being followed. Customers are not dupes who need excessive protection, they are equal partners in a deal whose terms are constantly changing.

HHCL+Partners go on to argue that too much of traditional advertising and advertising theory is about one-way communication – about the brand owner *selling* to consumers. They argue that the role of 'brand communication' (which they suggest includes, but is not exclusively, advertising) should be about two-way conversation.

> *Communication is about listening as well as talking.*

They suggest that the role of brand communication should be to establish and build a relationship with its users, that the purchase is not the end of the sale but rather the beginning of a relationship, that brand purchase can be likened to an application to join a club.

While at first this can seem a little far-fetched, HHCL+ Partners point to 'My first Sony' which they call "*the first step on the ladder of membership*", British Airways and its Executive Club and the fact that over 80 per cent of all American branded goods now carry a freephone number so that their consumers, no their customers, can contact them directly.

If a brand can stand for certain values, can have a distinct personality then why shouldn't you have an on-going 'relationship' with it? Why else has Procter & Gamble built up a massive database of the details of some 44 million consumers?

There are two other main reasons why brands may choose not to advertise in the future, or at least not as much. The first of these is the cost of advertising.

The cost of advertising has increased enormously over the last 40 years at a rate well ahead of the rate of inflation. If you wanted to buy one 30 second commercial in the centre break of *Coronation Street* across the network (in all the regions of the country) it would cost you something like £100,000. A single-page, black and white ad in *The Sun* on one specific day would cost around £30,000. A 30-second commercial on national American TV in the Superbowl can cost over US$1.25 million!

While brands' advertising budgets are large, as the cost of advertising continues to spiral even their budgets don't go anywhere near as far as they did in the past. To take just one example, Guinness spent over £10 million on advertising in the UK in 1997 – that's an awful lot of pints that need to be sold to pay for it. If they are to continue buying the same real level of exposure they will need more and more money as every year passes.

Brand building with advertising is not cheap and it isn't getting any cheaper. In fact, a number of big brand companies have been rationalising the number of brands they have and support . For example, Unilever sold Fray Bentos to Campbell Foods.

The other main reason why brands may choose not to advertise is the proliferation of new and different channels of communication which provide alternative media with which the brand can communicate with its customers. Its not that they won't communicate, it's just that they will find new ways of doing it. Four examples of these 'new media' would be:

The Internet	A 'free' medium through which any brand can communicate with potential customers anywhere around the world, so long as they are linked up to the web.
Brand Magazines	A brand's own magazine where it controls not just the advertising but the editorial as well and if the magazine is good enough it can charge for it too.
Brand Worlds	Turning your brand into an experience – a three dimensional world. Again the best of these are so good that consumers will happily pay to visit them.
Product Placement	The selection and placement of your brand in an appropriate piece of entertainment, e.g. film or television series. In the UK it is illegal to pay for placement on television but not so in films. BMW were one of the many brands who paid to have their brand included in the James Bond movie *Tomorrow Never Dies*.

In fact, in an increasingly multi-media world there are an increasing number of brands that have been built with little or no traditional advertising – consider The Body Shop and Marks & Spencer, both retailers who have used their shops, their lorries and public relations to great effect.

In conclusion, the reason why brands advertised was traditionally to sell to us, the consumers. Now it may be to build a relationship with us the customers. Whichever view is correct, and there is truth in both, brands advertise because advertising is a powerful tool with which to create and maintain a true 'brand'.

But perhaps with the recent and on-going changes to our world the question for the future will be not "Why do brands advertise?" but rather "Should brands use advertising as part of their total communication or rely on other forms of media?"

Whose Brand Is It Anyway?

Bird's Eye? World Cuisine? Menumaster? An example of complicated brand architecture. (See chapter three: Are there different types of branding?)

Experiencing the Brand

In the future we will want to be more involved with the brands we like. (See chapter eighteen: What does the future hold?)

The Branding Iron

Branding has come a long way since its origins as a mark of ownership. (See chapter two: What are the origins of branding?)

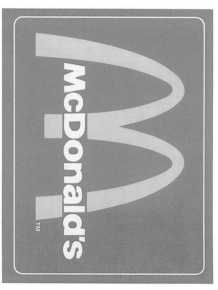

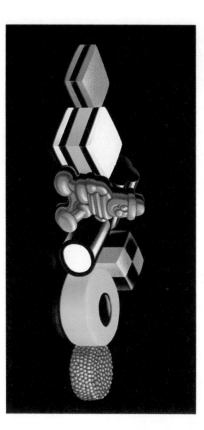

McDonald's M

Mother McDonald's breasts? (See chapter eight: What are brand icons and what roles do they play?)

Bertie Bassett

"One sometimes finds what one is not looking for." (Fleming)Liquorice Allsorts were created by accident.(See chapter two: What are the origins of branding?)

Betty Crocker Portraits

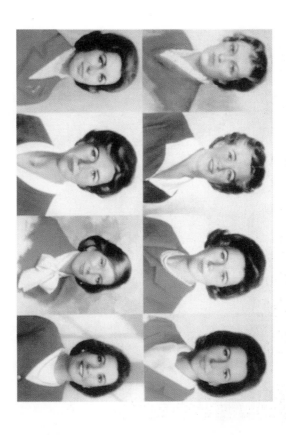

Betty Crocker has given her name to a range of home baking products, had her portrait painted nine times, spoken on the radio and written several cookery books, yet she doesn't exist. (See chapter six: How do brands get their names?)

Have You Been Tango'd?
(See chapter ten: Why do brands advertise?)

WE'RE BIG ENOUGH TO SAY WE'RE N°4

Photo: John Claridge

TO OUR
MEMBERS WE'RE
THE 4TH
EMERGENCY
SERVICE

The Fourth Emerceny Service

From being those very nice men who helped when your car broke down the AA has re-positioned itself as 'The Fourth Emercency Service'. (See chapter nine: What is brand positioning and where does it fit into the marketing mix?)

11

How do brands grow?

Brands are big business (for just how big, see chapter fifteen) and the aim of most businesses is to make money, as much money as possible. Therefore most businesses want their brands to grow as this will mean more sales, more turnover and more profit.

There is, however, a small but important minority of companies that do not conform to this stereotype, including businesses such as charities and mutual building societies. However, even many of these companies will depend on their brands being successful and growing if they are to achieve their aims in this increasingly competitive world.

Take charities. They are competing with other charities for our donations and competing with everything else, all the other brands and activities on which we could be spending our money. It's no wonder then that many of the big charities have in recent years focused on the marketing of their brands.

There have been many re-launches with new names, new logos and increasingly sophisticated marketing campaigns. What was Dr Barnardo's is now simply Barnardo's, what was The Spastics Society is now Scope. They want their brand, their charity, to appeal to you. They want to encourage you to donate to them rather than to other charities or rather than spending the money on other profit making brands.

So nearly all companies, whatever their objectives, want their brands to grow; and there are three main ways in which a brand can grow.

♦ *Organic Growth*

The 'base' brand (and product) can get bigger. The original brand becomes more popular or the same brand is used more frequently and sales therefore increase.

♦ *Growth through Line Extension*

The brand can offer new versions of itself within its existing market e.g. new flavours or variants

♦ *Growth through Brand Extension*

The brand can use its 'franchise' – the well of goodwill based on the perceptions held by its customers – as a springboard to launch a new product, bearing its name, into a new category or market.

Within each of these three routes there are many ways and means by which the brands grow. This chapter will look at organic growth and line extensions while chapter twelve will explore the increasingly popular concept of brand extension.

Organic Growth

Sales of any one brand increase because what they have to offer becomes attractive to somebody, somewhere. The more 'somebodies' they attract the greater their growth will be.

As we have seen in previous chapters, a brand's offering is made up of a mixture of both functional and emotional elements. Functional aspects include such things as price and the product's ability to deliver its physical purpose. Emotional aspects include such factors as personality and image. Improving any one of these aspects, making it more attractive to more people can therefore lead to growth.

A price reduction, whether permanent or just a special offer, will generally increase sales, though not necessarily profit. Indeed in the case of a special offer it could just be encouraging those people who already buy it to stock up on it while the price is cheaper. If this is all that happened then there would be no long-term growth for the brand but rather a short-term blip offset by a corresponding decline in sales when the offer price ends. However, the first rule of economics, namely that demand increases as price decreases all other things being equal, means that there is generally at least some volume growth from a price cut.

A powerful advertising campaign can also boost sales as was discussed in chapter ten. Increasing the brand's availability, so more people have the chance to buy it or buy

it on more occasions, can significantly increase sales.

In fact, Coca-Cola's distribution is one of the cornerstones of that brand's success. Coca-Cola's promise of "Always" in its current advertising is a reflection of the brand's long standing business mission "to always be within arms reach of *desire*". Its foreign sales department dates back to 1926 but it was the Second World War and the spread of American GIs that were the real driving force behind the spread of Coca-Cola. Everywhere the GIs went, Coke was sure to follow.

Nowadays, Coca-Cola's distribution is phenomenal – not only is it available from Atlanta to Zanzibar, from Moscow to Melbourne but you can buy it at supermarkets, at newsagents, at your local garage, at the cinema, in restaurants, at street corners, at cafes, at football matches, at pop concerts and increasingly you can even buy it from vending machines in car parks and at schools.

When Neil Armstrong and his fellow Apollo XI astronauts returned from the first moon landing, they were greeted by a neon sign in Times Square that read:

Welcome back to Earth, home of Coca-Cola.

Whilst there are, therefore, numerous marketing tools to help achieve organic growth, this type of growth stems from one of three things: getting that brand used by more people, getting it used by the same people more often or getting people to use more of it on any of the occasions they use it in the first place.

In today's highly developed marketplace with the large numbers of existing and competing brands this can be easier than it sounds. One company, however, that has been very successful in growing its established brands through organic growth is Kellogg's. Many of the most famous Kellogg's brands like Corn Flakes, Rice Krispies and Frosties were launched at the beginning or early part of this century. Sales have built up over the years but Kellogg's is still keen to find further growth as the recent strategies adopted by their brands demonstrate.

Kellogg's Frosties' primary appeal has traditionally been amongst children. Tony the Tiger, the *'secret sugar frosting'* and the *"they're grrrrr – reat!"* slogan are all aspects of how the brand has been developed and have been used to appeal to kids over the years.

However, more recently Kellogg's has started to target adults – a group who haven't traditionally consumed the brand in large amounts. They have used advertising, PR and the other brand marketing tools to remind an older generation of just how enjoyable Frosties are and how adults can eat them too. If Kellogg's can get both children and adults to eat and enjoy the brand then more people will be eating the brand, more will be sold and the brand will grow.

Kellogg's have adopted a different approach with their flagship brand, Corn Flakes. At nearly a hundred years old they don't expect to grow the brand further do they? Hasn't everyone who is going to try the brand already tried it? Well Kellogg's obviously believe there's life in the old brand yet!

By now, everyone should know that Kellogg's believe their Corn Flakes are the *'sunshine taste'* and that they're great for breakfast. Most of us have eaten, and indeed many still eat them for breakfast. However, over the last five to ten years, Kellogg's have mounted an increasingly successful campaign to get us to eat Kellogg's Corn Flakes as an evening or even tea-time snack. They may not be able to tempt many more of us to have them for breakfast but they can encourage those who do like them to eat them more often.

Actually Kellogg's Corn Flakes also fits the mould of a brand trying to find more users. Having found a large group of 'converts' to Dr Kellogg's *'right living'* diet in one country, Kellogg's have recognised that another way to grow the brand is to take your brand to new countries and try and recruit some new converts. And, surprising though it may seem, more and more French people are now forsaking their croissants and enjoying a bowl of Corn Flakes for breakfast.

The final variation on organic growth is to encourage consumers to use 'more', that is more of the brand at any occasion when they are already using the brand. Staying in the cereal market, what was the thinking behind Shredded Wheat's challenge *"I bet you can't eat three?"* if not an encouragement to have just one *more*?

There is an apocryphal story, and I must stress *a story* because I have no proof it is true, that a manufacturer of baby powder developed a strategy to increase its sales by selling 'more'.

The *story* goes that after a period of sales remaining broadly static, the baby powder management team was set the challenge of returning the brand to growth. This led them to a fundamental review of all aspects of the brand. Its name, its formulation, its pricing, its advertising, the competition…and finally how it was used.

Having nearly finished this review and having discovered nothing significant, an in-depth research study was undertaken to look at how the brand was actually used in consumers' homes. It was during this study that a keen young brand manager is said to have noticed a peculiar but amazing consistent trait amongst the brand's users. Almost every mother who used the baby powder did two quick shakes of the bottle and then spread the powder that had come out over their baby's bottom. Now different mothers shook the powder in different ways and got different amounts of powder out, but they all shook the bottle twice.

Based on this observation, the brand manager's ingenious suggestion was both simple and devious. He suggested that they made the holes in the top of their baby powder bottle bigger – 50 per cent bigger. This meant that if every mother continued with the instinctive 'two shake' method of powdering their baby's bottom, more powder would come out every time and each bottle would be used up more frequently. Mothers would use more without even realising it. The *story* is that sales went up nearly 30 per cent following the increase in hole size!

So, in summary, there are three main ways in which organic growth occurs – more people use the brand, the same people use it more often or more of the product is used on any one occasion.

It is important to realise that organic growth for one brand is often at the expense of another brand. If two brands are competing in the same market for the same customer then one brand's gain is another brand's loss. If I buy a shampoo and choose to buy a Wash'n'Go rather than a Head and Shoulders and my choice is mirrored by thousands of others then Wash'n'Go will grow and Head and Shoulders will shrink.

Whilst this seems obvious, it is important because often a company may own more than one brand in any one market. Indeed both Wash'n'Go and Head and Shoulders are owned by Procter & Gamble. Therefore the aim of these multi-brand companies may not be focused on the sale of any one brand but rather on taking a larger share of the market with its portfolio of brands.

Growth through Line Extension

Whilst organic growth essentially comes from selling more and more of the *same* branded product, growth through line extension comes from selling more and more of *similar* products.

A line extension is defined as being a variant of the same basic product. It might be a new flavour or a new size. The reason for producing them, however, is the same, more varieties for more growth. Growth that comes via those same basic means of either encouraging more people to buy your brand or the same people to buy it more often or just more of it.

Take for example Oxo. Oxo was originally only available in beef flavour. Indeed the original Oxo (beef) cube was launched in 1910 and it wasn't until the 1960s that Chicken Oxo was launched. Now the brand is available in a range of flavours including vegetable and lamb.

Having a range of flavours encourages people to use Oxo more often. They can use the beef cube on Monday when they are cooking steak and kidney pie and they can use Oxo again on Wednesday but this time the chicken variety as they might be cooking coq au vin.

Varieties can encourage more or new people to use a brand too. When Oxo launched their vegetable cube in 1989 it encouraged increased usage amongst existing buyers, as they used it in vegetable dishes. However it also attracted new users to Oxo – vegetarians who until then couldn't use any Oxo because of the real meat stock content. Oxo's vegetable stock cubes are approved by the Vegetarian Society as they are completely meat free and so vegetarians can now happily buy at least one version of the same brand.

Very few brands nowadays are pure 'one product, one brand' brands. Most brands have been line extended in some shape or form.

In some markets line extension has now almost become an epidemic – there are so many varieties and variations that as a consumer it is incredibly difficult to know what product you are supposed to choose. Take for example the toothpaste market. In the 'old' days if you wanted Colgate all you had to do was decide what tube size you wanted. Nowadays the choice is almost bewildering. Nowadays the choice is between:

◆ Regular

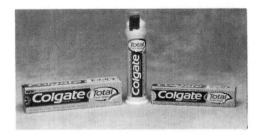

◆ Total

◆ My First Colgate

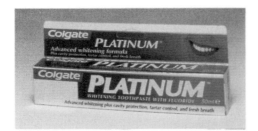

♦ Platinum

♦ Deep Clean

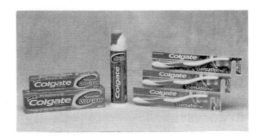

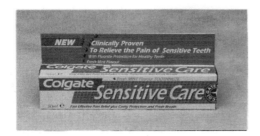

♦ Sensitive Care

12

What is brand extension and why is it so popular?

Nowadays you can buy an ice-cream from Mars, lipsticks from Oil of Ulay and sweatshirts from Lego. You can even open a bank account at Tesco or get coloured condoms from Bennetton.

All these brands were originally much more focused in their offering. Mars was a chocolate bar, Oil of Ulay was just a moisturiser and Lego made toys. Tesco was a grocery supermarket and Bennetton sold clothes. Yet now they all wish to compete in new markets with different products or services. In the words of the old Irving Berlin song *"heaven knows, anything goes"*.

Brand extension, the use (and occasional misuse) of an existing brand name and equity to launch a product or service into a category or market not normally associated with that brand, has in recent years become one of the most potent forces behind existing brand growth. In fact it seems like 'have brand, will travel' should be the buzzwords for brand growth in the 1980s and the 1990s.

While a line extension offers the customer more varieties or styles of the original brand in its original market, a brand extension takes an existing brand to pastures new.

So taking Mars as an example we can see that the original chocolate bar has been line extended into different styles including Mars Kingsize, Mars Miniatures and for limited periods Dark Chocolate Mars. However, when Mars launched the Mars ice cream, it entered a new market for that brand and as such had extended the brand franchise. Mars has also brand extended into the flavoured milk drinks market with Mars in a bottle.

So why has brand extension become so popular in recent years?

The main reason is that it is notoriously difficult and expensive to launch a completely new brand. The most often quoted statistic being that nine out of every ten new brands fail. New brands are therefore seen as a high risk, though sometimes high return, strategy.

Brand extension is seen as a cheaper and more reliable method of building on what already exists. Not surprisingly, companies who will already have invested a lot of money in creating a brand are keen to maximise any successful brand's full potential. They want to leverage the initial success of that brand and exploit the equity they have established with it.

With a brand extension there is already awareness of the brand name and consequently it may be possible to reduce expenditure on advertising when establishing the new product. There may be economies of scale with distribution, the sales force and even research and development.

A brand extension builds on what is already there, a new brand often has to build from scratch.

That's why you don't just get Pampers Nappies but Pampers Babywipes as well. It's why Pantene is not just available as shampoos but conditioners and hair sprays as well. It's why you can now buy Colgate mouthwash and Colgate toothbrushes, as well as all those line extensions mentioned a few pages earlier.

One other reason why brands have extended is to maintain their ability to advertise their products. As restrictions on cigarette advertising have become increasingly tight, a number of tobacco manufacturers have extended their brands into new categories where they may still be able to advertise even after a ban on cigarette advertising is imposed. Dunhill is now known as a prestige brand rather than just a cigarette brand. Marlboro has extended into clothing and holidays.

There is a story that, in France, Marlboro launched matches and lighters as a means of getting around a ban on cigarette advertising. It is said they spent more on advertising them than they could possibly have made in profit until the French government spotted the wheeze and closed the loophole.

However, brand extension is not always the answer.

History is littered with brand extension failures. Do you remember Kellogg's Rise and Shine, their instant fruit breakfast drink? Do you remember Ribena Fruit and Fibre Juice?

Statistics on the success rate of brand extensions are difficult to find, especially as what constitutes a 'success' varies enormously. However, in one survey, OC&C used a simple but effective definition of success – still being on the shelves six years after launch – and estimated that five out of every ten brand extensions fail.

The Timotei Skincare range is an example of where a brand extension seemed, at first, a sensible idea but ultimately proved a financial disaster. Timotei was first launched in 1975 in Sweden. It was a major success and Unilever, the company that owned the brand, exported the mix – name, packaging, product and advertising – all around the world.

The brand was launched in the UK in 1982. Despite having what appeared to be a meaningless name, it was an instant success. In fact, the name Timotei comes from the Finnish word for pasture which for a mild shampoo made with natural herb extracts and with an idyllic, outdoor image of the countryside is entirely appropriate.

The brand was successful in the UK for a number of reasons. The penetration of showers had been increasing throughout the 1970s and with it so had been the frequency with which people washed their hair. This had led to some concern that we had been over-washing our hair with the then current 'strong' shampoos. We, the consumers, were to welcome a shampoo that claimed it was so mild that you can wash your hair as often as you want.

Another factor in its success was that the early 1980s was a period when the environmental, green movement grew stronger and a 'natural' shampoo would seem increasingly appealing. Finally the advertising with its powerful brand icons of the blonde lady and the beautiful 'Timoteiland' were to prove highly distinctive and motivating.

The brand grew rapidly to become the number two brand in the market (behind the then brand leader – Head and Shoulders). It established a set of brand values for itself that included naturalness, mildness, simplicity, beauty, frequency of use and the inclusion of herb extracts.

In the mid-1980s when Unilever was looking at ways of building its presence in the skincare market, it therefore seemed obvious that Timotei was a brand whose equity could be extended.

Indeed initial consumer research showed that a mid-market range of skincare products would be entirely consistent and appropriate for the Timotei brand. So in 1986, the Timotei skincare range of cleanser, moisturiser and revitaliser were launched. They were supported by television and press advertising.

However, sales were disappointing and the products were quickly dropped. Why had Timotei failed? The key reason was that, while Timotei's brand values of mildness, naturalness, simplicity and beauty were all relevant and credible for this new market, they weren't distinctive.

There were already a number of brands in the market that offered all these attributes. They included The Body Shop, Simple and, the similarly named, Pure and Simple. Timotei offered nothing new. So while the Timotei products were reasonably priced and of a good quality they weren't offering anything new, different or appealing enough to make consumers change their existing buying habits and brand loyalties.

The moral of this tale is that while new brand development might be high risk and expensive, brand extension is not without its own risks and costs. Not all brand extensions succeed and similarly not all brand extensions follow the same pattern. Different brands extend in different ways.

Perhaps the most obvious way is to extend the brand on some aspect of the original product, whether this is an ingredient or a special flavour. For example, Ribena was originally a blackcurrant squash which you diluted with water. Nowadays you can get everything from sparkling Ribena in a can, which competes with other carbonated drinks, to a frozen blackcurrant Ribena water ice, which competes with other ice-cream brands like Calipso.

All these Ribena extensions remain true to the 'blackcurrant-ness' of the original product. Indeed where they have moved away from blackcurrant to other fruit flavours, as in their orange Fruit and Fibre Juice, they have been less successful.

All the Mars brand extensions mentioned earlier in this chapter, the ice-cream and the drink offer the total Mars product proposition of chocolate, glucose and caramel, only they do it in alternative product categories.

Brands can extend not just on the product features but on the benefits they offer. Lucozade was originally a glucose based drink. However, the functional benefit it claims to deliver is energy. On this basis line extending into sports drinks and brand extending into energy tablets are both reasonable ways of growing the brand.

An alternative basis for a brand extension is to build on the brand's image. This relies on a brand's ability to be a desirable badge. You can buy Guinness, the famous Irish stout brand, not only as a drink but as clothing. Indeed the first Guinness clothing store opened in Dublin in 1997. Interestingly, this can allow people who like the Guinness brand but not the stout to buy into the brand.

However, perhaps the brand that has been most successful at brand extension is Disney. Each of its films is like a sub-brand and Disney exploits each film's potential to add appeal and value to a whole range of products. Some of these they produce and sell themselves but many of them are produced and sold by other companies who buy the licence from Disney for that particular brand.

In a recent article in *The New Yorker* magazine it was claimed there were as many as 17,000 different products based on the *101 Dalmatians* film alone. You can get T-shirts, stuffed toys, computer games, chocolates, yoghurts, biscuits, party hats. In fact if you put all those products together it would probably fill a medium-sized supermarket!

As we have seen brands have their own values and personalities. In many cases these values are not specific to a particular sector or category. They are benefits that cross categories and products. A good example of this is Virgin. The Virgin brand stretches from the cola market to the music industry, from the airline business to financial services, from trains to cosmetics.

These can appear to be a wildly disparate set of markets which have nothing in common. However, once you realise that Virgin is not based on any one product but a set of values then a pattern can start to emerge. As Richard Branson said himself in an interview with *Marketing Week* magazine:

> *There is little to hold the companies together except the Virgin brand, but we do have the brand and we can license it to a diverse group of interests.*

Virgin positions itself as an the non-conventional consumers' champion who will take on big, established and 'establishment' businesses wherever it feels it can offer the people a better alternative and make a profit for itself.

Hence they will take on British Airways and offer a package which they claim makes flying more enjoyable by offering services that include a personal video screen and ice creams served during the movies. They will take on Coca-Cola and offer a product which they say tastes just as good but doesn't cost as much because it doesn't need so much advertising or such a high profit margin! They will take on the banking and financial institutes offering PEPs without the middleman (and his fees) and speak in plain English.

One final method of growing your brand through brand extension is to take advantage of a 'captive' audience or a brand-consumer relationship that has been established.

Hence most of the bank brands have extended their offers to include mortgages, insurance and pensions. They know you and your financial situation, or at least they should, and so can offer other associated products to suit your needs.

A number of retailer brands like Tesco's and Sainsbury's have also based extensions like moving into pharmacies, dry-cleaning and banking on providing these other services conveniently, under the same roof, while you are, albeit willingly, their captive audience.

Looking forward, brand extension is likely to continue to be a significant means of creating brand growth as it is both a practical and flexible means of exploiting the equity built up in a brand, even if it isn't foolproof and as Will Whitehorn, Corporate Affairs Director for the Virgin group, said:

> *The brand transcends any one product.*

13

Where do new brands come from?

Fifty years ago, many of today's big brands didn't exist. There was no Microsoft or Apple. There was no One2One or Orange. All of which means that in fifty years time there will probably be a holographic entertainment company called Blackcurrant and a space travel brand called Mango!

More seriously, what Apple and Orange, Microsoft, One2One, Sun MicroSystems, Vodaphone and a whole host of other brands demonstrate is that technology is one of the most fertile sources there is when it comes to the creation of new brands. As Steve Jobs, co-founder of Apple, has been quoted as saying:

> *Every time a technology window opens there is an opportunity completely to re-invent an industry.*

The development and application of new technology allows companies to do new things or, indeed, to do old things better. They can then offer us, their consumers, new or improved benefits whether that is a practical, user-friendly personal computer or the ability to be in contact with friends and colleagues wherever we are.

Then, in the case of existing companies, it is their decision whether they launch these new products or services as new brands in their own right, new sub-brands related to existing brands or simply as an improved version of an already existing brand.

When Unilever developed Glucasil, the first nutrient that actively nourished the roots of the hair, they chose to launch it in a completely new brand, Organics. When Sony developed the technology for miniature, personal and highly portable stereos, they chose to launch them as a sub-brand,

Walkman, but kept it closely related to the parent brand, Sony. It became a world-wide success as Sony Walkman. However, when Colgate Palmolive developed ZCT as a new active ingredient for toothpaste, they decided not to launch a new brand of any sort, rather they re-launched their existing brand, Colgate, as new and improved.

If it is a new company, then it is not surprisingly a new brand or brands that are created. Microsoft was a new company and it has become a brand in its own right, as have many of its products like Windows and Encarta.

If new technology epitomises the completely new and is one extreme of a new brand development spectrum, then the opposite extreme, which is equally if not more popular, is the 'me-too' or copycat brand.

As the name suggests a 'me-too' brand is a brand created to follow and mimic another brand. It imitates the original in terms of its functionality and indeed also often copies it in terms of its positioning, brand name and even graphic design.

Is any similarity with Planet Hollywood
purely incidental?

Having seen the success of a new brand, another brand (or brands) follows it into the market with a similar offering hoping it will capture a share of the success. The recent explosion of alcopop brands is a perfect example of this phenomenon. The initial success of the Two Dogs and Hooch brands was rapidly followed by a whole host of 'me-too' brands as companies scrambled to get a share of a rapidly growing sector.

In instances where, instead of just one 'me-too' brand, there are several, the additional brands are known as 'me-threes', 'me-fours' and 'me-fives' and where a copy arrives some time after the original it may well be a 'me-too-late '!

The practice of 'me-too-ing' offers the companies who use it a low-cost, low-risk means of entering a market. Given the high-risk, high-cost reputation of new brand development and the high levels of failure it is not surprising that it is such a popular strategy.

However, in many cases these 'me-toos' aren't created to be brands in their own right. They are just products. They won't have their own values or personalities that distinguish a brand from a product. In fact, there is often never any intention to develop a separate positioning or a distinctive personality for them. They are designed to live off the new brand or at least to live in its shadow.

In these cases the 'me-too' products will normally be sold under the umbrella of an existing brand. Perhaps the most obvious and the most prevalent example of this type of 'me-too-ing' occurs in many food and drink markets. The major companies who are producing these 'me-too' products are the big retail brands – Sainsbury's, Tesco, Asda and Safeway.

These retailers watch and monitor the performance of new brands as they enter the market and if the brand is successful they will approach other manufacturers to produce a version of that brand for them to be sold under their own brand name.

Given that these 'me-toos' are not designed to be brands they have to find an edge, a point of difference against the original brand if they are to succeed. They have to do something to make themselves attractive to us, the consumers. Often this point of difference will be a lower price.

The retail brands haven't had the cost of all the initial

exploratory research and development and don't usually have the cost of advertising their version of a brand so they can afford to charge less. From the consumer's point of view this can be good news, we can get a good quality version of the product we want for less money and as we have seen in an earlier chapter we are increasingly happy to take this option.

So while imitation may be the sincerest form of flattery, it can be a pain in the neck if you are a brand owner trying to create and build a new brand.

This competition between the traditional manufacturer brands and the lower-priced, 'me-too' products sold under a retailer's branding is one of the most important issues in the evolution of modern branding. The battle between brands' and retailers' own label products probably occupies more space in marketing media than any other subject. Indeed it will take up more space in this book as some of the implications for the future of branding are discussed in chapter eighteen.

A final variation on the 'me-too' brand is the 'me-one' brand. These are created when one company sees a successful brand operating in one area or country and 'copies the idea' so it can launch it onto its own home market. In that market this new brand appears to be an original, not a 'me-too'. In reality, if viewed globally, it is another copy. It is however known as 'me-one'.

It can be a highly successful strategy as the case of the Wall's Magnum brand demonstrates. In the USA a confectionery brand, Dove, developed a brand-extension and entered the ice-cream market with what was to all intents and purposes a giant choc-ice on a stick. Dove ice-cream was a large, premium ice-cream centre coated in real milk chocolate and presented as a lolly. Though priced at a significant premium compared to most of its competition it was a major success.

A short while later Wall's launched Magnum onto the UK market. It was a large, premium ice cream centre coated in real milk chocolate and on a stick. It too has been a major success which just goes to prove yet again that though we like to think we are different from the Americans we are surprisingly alike in many ways!

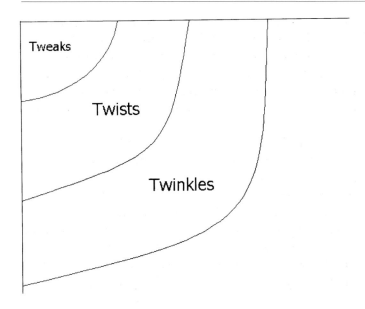

Paul Walton and Thom Braun, of the marketing consultants The Value Engineers, have argued that innovation (of which new brand creation is one part) can be broadly segmented into three types, namely tweaks, twists and twinkles. They suggest that these 3Ts:

> . . . *form a spectrum within which all (product) innovations can be placed. At one end, Twinkles represent high-risk, high-added-value initiatives. At the other end, Tweaks represent low-risk, low-added-value changes to what already exists in the market place.*

The application of new technology to create a new brand can therefore be seen as a twinkle and a 'me-too' brand can be seen as a tweak. Twists are a middle ground, based on clever rearrangements of what already exists. Like twinkles and tweaks, twists can also be the base of new brand creation. Walton and Braun quote the case of Pepsi Max as an example.

> *Pepsi Max could not be considered a Twinkle. As a carbonated cola drink in a can, it sticks very much to the delivery system rules of the soft drinks market. In several important respects, however, Pepsi Max is a great deal more than a Tweak. Cola market Tweaks*

can be characterised by the various cherry-flavoured and caffeine-free versions that have been launched by the major branded manufacturers. In each case, the new product is clearly positioned as a marginal variant of the mainstream brand. The business expectations are often matched by the marketing investment levels, and in most cases both are low.

Pepsi Max was different because it rearranged the way consumers saw the market. It was a market with two main segments: 'original' colas (drunk predominately by men who claimed to want a fuller taste) and 'diet' colas (drunk largely by women who preferred the sugar-free option). Against this market background, PepsiCo realised that they could make a bold assault on the status quo by positioning a sugar-free cola as a fuller-flavour drink targeted at young men. Although sugar-free, it would not focus on being less of something (i.e. 'diet'), but rather on being more of something (i.e. 'the max').

The immediate success of Pepsi Max took it well beyond what might have been achieved by a simple Tweak. Indeed, the brand effectively re-segmented the market to suit its own strengths and thereby created a new mainstream opportunity.

Another source of new brand development is the drive, ambition or indeed the beliefs of an individual. Two examples that are just over a hundred years apart, both demonstrate just how important one person can be in the creation of a brand.

Thomas Richard Allinson was only fifteen when he left home in 1873 to become a chemist's assistant. Using the money he earned and with some help from his grandfather he went on to study medicine at Edinburgh University where his keen interest in people's diet developed.

He qualified as a doctor and moved to London where he set up his own practice in 1888. He was already a keen advocate of the benefits of wholemeal flour and indeed wrote a book entitled *The Advantages of Wholemeal Bread*. His other books included such gripping titles as *A System for Hygienic*

Medicine and *Rheumatism* as well as the much more intriguingly titled *Book for Married Women*.

However, at this point in history there were very few mills that produced high quality wholemeal flour so yet again demonstrating his drive and his clear passion for all things wholemeal he founded the "Natural Food Company" in 1892 and bought a small mill of his own in Bethnal Green.

He started selling the flour, now bearing his name, to bakers and went on to provide them with certificates stating that they were making bread to his standard. His brand grew and grew. In 1921 the company acquired a new mill in Castleford where to this day it produces stone-ground, wholemeal flour to the same high standards Dr Thomas Allinson established for his brand at its birth.

Just over 100 years after Thomas Allinson left home the imminent departure of another man led to the establishment of another brand. The man about to depart was Gordon Roddick. He was leaving for an expedition which was to take him from Buenos Aires to New York on horseback.

His young wife, Anita, needed the means to support herself and their young family while he was away and she decided that she wanted to open a shop selling cosmetics. However, it was to be no ordinary cosmetics shop, she wanted to follow the practice of Tahitian women who made cosmetics using local, natural products.

The name of her new enterprise, this new brand, was 'The Body Shop'. Roddick had seen the name in America at a car bodywork garage and had immediately liked it.

The name wasn't popular with two undertakers who had premises close to the first store in Brighton. They thought the name might be bad for their trade, but when they sent her a solicitor's letter she turned it to good effect by contacting the local paper and gaining herself and her new brand some free publicity.

On Saturday 27 March 1976, The Body Shop opened its doors to the public for the first time. The first day's takings were £130. The Body Shop now has more than 1,650 stores worldwide and the brand is an international success.

Ideas for new brands can and do come from anywhere and it is true to say that not all new brands are the result of careful planning. As Sir Alexander Fleming once said:

One sometimes finds what one is not looking for.

While in his case this was penicillin, there are a number of notable cases where serendipity played a major role in the creation of a new brand. For example, when the scientists at 3M invented a new substance that had the characteristics of being a weak but inexhaustible adhesive which could be used repeatedly without leaving a trace they had no idea how to use it. Millions and millions of Post-it Notes later, 3M are exceptionally glad they found something they weren't looking for.

The inspiration for the Viennetta brand is said to have come to a Wall's executive when his wife gave him a mille feuilles cream cake, so look around you carefully, the next new brand idea may be closer than you think.

14

What makes a successful brand?

Identifying a brand that will be a major future success is not as easy as it might at first seem. It is rather like spotting a future star, and show business is full of stories, such as the man who turned down The Beatles and the studio who thought *ET* wouldn't appeal to anyone over the age of eight.

It is easier to analyse a number of already successful brands and identify some of the key traits they have in common. Not surprisingly given the parallel between brands and stars, the traits that mark out a true superstar are often the same ones that mark out the really successful brands. What some have called the '*superbrands*'!

Both are big and while size is important, in so far as it reflects success, it is also true to say that size isn't everything. Indeed if you look at a number of brands as well as a number of stars, they have actually had less success than you might have originally thought. For both stars and brands it can be the case that they have a much stronger position in the minds of consumers than the reality suggests. Oxo has a much bigger status than its turnover might suggest. Julia Roberts has appeared in more turkeys than she has starred in blockbusters.

What both successful brands and stars can command is instant recognition. They own a space in our minds. Their appearances, and key images of them, have become cultural icons. Whether it's the shape of the Coca-Cola bottle or the image of Humphrey Bogart and Ingrid Bergman in *Casablanca* they are known all around the world.

Superstars like Bogart and Bergman are often described as having 'it', that indefinable something that makes all the difference. Marlon Brando is undoubtedly a very fine actor but he also has 'it'. He does what is expected of him yet still manages to give that little bit more. He has that something extra that has helped create an aura about him and gives him a special appeal. He isn't just an actor, he's a star.

Brands can have 'it' as well but in a brand this translates to the intangible benefits it can offer, benefits over and above tangible, rational benefits like quality. This doesn't mean quality isn't important, indeed it is a vital element in any brand's success.

Take Kellogg's for example. Kellogg's is a company that is absolutely committed to product quality. Reputedly they blind test their famous Corn Flakes against other leading brands and retailers' own brands every six months and if any of their competitors are better or even just as good as Kellogg's then they work on their product until it is improved to beat all comers. If so, there is substance to their claim to be *"the original and best"*.

However, as we have seen, quality like beauty, is in the eye of the beholder and people's perceptions of quality can, and do, vary enormously. Quality isn't usually enough, if that is all that is on offer. There are hundreds of very fine actors who will never be stars, they don't have 'it'.

As David Arnold describes in his *Handbook of Brand Management*, a successful brand:

> *. . .will offer intangible benefits over and above the product. To elicit loyalty, a brand must offer some intangible benefits. These are usually referred to as values.*

> *The delights of watching Lendl play against Agassi at tennis is more than just watching the angle and pace of the shots. The contrast between characters, styles and approaches to the game is what involves the crowd.*

> *It is the same with products. Levi jeans offer the values of toughness, informality and American-ness, whereas Gucci jeans offer style and a cosmopolitan image. These personalities are the stock in trade of branding. Personality is a benefit, as the price premium of leading brands over the decades demonstrates.*

So successful brands must have 'it'. They will have a special appeal, a unique energy that you can almost feel. Virgin has 'it', Nike has 'it'.

True success is not just a flash in the pan. True stars aren't one hit wonders. Successful brands have longevity. In the case of superstars this longevity is reflected in the appeal they still have long after their, often untimely, deaths. In the case of brands, their appeal can outlive their creators and they can have a life that is well in excess of any of their particular products.

Unfortunately Marilyn Monroe died young yet her appeal lives on. Ford no longer makes the Model T but the brand is far from dead. Walt Disney died in 1966 but the Disney brand is now bigger than ever.

One of the most widely quoted theories of marketing is that products have a lifecycle.

Figure of a Product Lifecycle

Volume

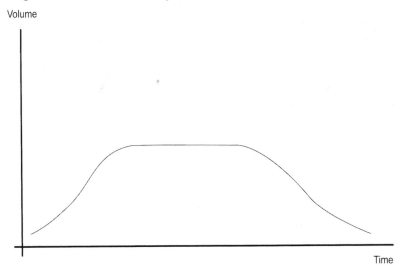

Time

The theory is that products go through four distinct phases. An initial phase following introduction, where the brand slowly starts to gain acceptance. It can be a period of high costs, low revenue and low profits as the product establishes itself on the market. Then it goes through a period of rapid growth where sales and profits quickly rise. The third phase is that of maturity where sales plateau. While it is the period of highest sales it can be a period of declining profits as competitive products enter the market and prices tend to fall. Finally the product moves into a period of decline and decay as consumers move away to newer, better products. Sales and profit drop away.

Now the length of any product lifecycle varies, especially the mature phase, but however long it is there is always an end in sight, or so goes the theory. (Although perhaps someone forgot to explain it to the Mars bar, Coca-Cola or Kellogg's Corn Flakes.)

In the case of a brand, which as we have seen can transcend any one product, this need not be the case. A brand's life can be extended through the launch of new products, whether they are line extensions and/or brand extensions. If the only product the Disney brand had was the *Steamboat Willie* film it is highly unlikely they would be the force they are in worldwide entertainment today.

Figure of a Brand Lifecycle: a series of product lifecycles

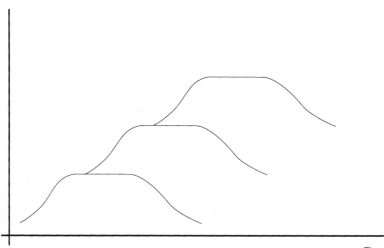

Thus a successful brand can outlive even the most successful product. In the UK it is reported that sales of Diet Coke are half that of the mighty original and full sugar Coca-Cola.

The superbrands tend to have been around for years and are very likely to be here in years to come. In summary, David Arnold concludes that a successful brand:

> . . .*must be a blend of complementary physical, rational and emotional appeals. The blend must be distinctive*

and result in a clear personality which will offer benefits of value to consumers.

What all this leads to is perhaps the truest measure of a successful brand – the notion of brand loyalty. That is the level of commitment consumers are willing to show for a brand.

For Tony Reilly, former CEO of H J Heinz, the:

> . . .*acid test on the issue (brand loyalty) is whether a housewife intending to buy Heinz Tomato Ketchup in a store, finding it to be out-of-stock, will walk out of the store to buy it elsewhere or switch to an alternative product.*

Other measures of brand loyalty would include how much we, the consumers, are willing to trust these brands. How much more are we willing to pay and go on paying for them versus any alternatives?

We have seen in chapter four that we trust a number of big, successful superbrands like Kellogg's and Heinz more than many of the country's institutions. We've seen that we are willing to pay and go on paying significant premiums for brands we like and value.

In fact we're increasingly joining brand clubs and becoming card carrying members of what have been called 'brand tribes or clans'. Whether that's the British Airways Executive Club, the Swatch Club, the *what* Lego Club or the Tesco Loyalty Card, they all represent groups of people who are willing to demonstrate their loyalty to their brand.

The labeling of Sony's kids range as 'my first Sony' demonstrates that Sony not only understands that children like their own things but includes the implicit assumption of a second, a third, a lifetime of Sonys.

Returning to our comparison between superbrands and superstars, there is an interesting parallel between these brand clubs and the fan clubs run on behalf of the stars. What's more we are not only joining these brand 'fan' clubs, we're buying the T-shirts as well! The Camel Collection is doing a roaring trade in branded merchandise. Camel branded polo shirts, sweatshirts, socks, umbrellas and much more besides are being sold, not given away, in a wide variety of stores.

People are proudly displaying their loyalty to their brands and it's not only Camel. It's an ever increasing number of brands from a Rowntree Fruit Pastilles pencil case to a Monopoly hankerchief, from a Coca-Cola mouse pad to their Murphy's T-shirts.

It is perhaps the ultimate ironic twist in this modern commercial world when we, the consumer, are paying our hard-earned money to become walking advertisements for brands. It may not be sensible or cool to wear your heart on your sleeve but we are happy to wear our brands on our chests. We are becoming a medium for brand messages and not only are we not getting paid for it, we are forking out considerable sums of our money for the privilege.

William Webb, an executive director of The Institute of Retail and Distribution Management, and a Scottish football fan, suggested at the 23rd AIDA Congress that this is merely an indication of what the really successful brands of the future are aiming to do. They want to replicate the level of commitment that a football fan feels for his club. They want people to be passionately committed to their brands. They want you to be their brand's advocate.

> *Simple brand loyalty is not enough. As competition gets tougher, brand owners are aiming for active advocacy wherein converts or 'brand clans' set out to convert the unconverted. This is really an extension of party plan or multi-level marketing, and The Body Shop is already employing it. People will feel as passionate about their allegiance to Safeway or Tesco as they do to Hibs or Hearts!*

You may think this all sounds a little far fetched until you speak to someone who has just got off their first Virgin Atlantic flight to the United States.

15

What is the world's most valuable brand?

Coca-Cola is the world's most famous brand. It is also, according to *Financial World*, the world's most valuable brand.

They valued the Coca-Cola brand in 1996, their 6th annual survey, at an estimated and truly amazing US$47,978 million or using the American definition $47 billion. At a conversion rate of £1 to US$1.60 that equates to £30,000 million give or take the odd 1,000 million.

To put that figure in some sort of perspective, it is more than the entire Gross Domestic Product (GDP) or "national output" of many nations.

Worth only US$343 million less was Marlboro, estimated at some US$47,635 million, while the third most valuable brand, worth a mere US$23,701 million, was the computer giant IBM.

The remaining brands in the top ten were:

4. McDonald's US$19,939 million;

5. Disney US$17,069 million;

6. Sony US$14,464 million;

7. Kodak US$14,442 million;

8. Intel US$13,274 million;

9. Gillette US$11,992 million;

10. Budweiser US$11,985 million.

That means the estimated total value of the top ten brands was more than *US$222,000,000,000* – and that's only the top ten!

It would appear that America leads the way in branding

as only one brand in the top ten is not American owned and that is 6th placed Sony. The next non-American brand is Nescafé which is estimated at US$10,337 million and ranks 14th. The most valuable wholly British brand is the Johnnie Walker whisky brand estimated at US$5,200 million and owned by Guinness. The Benson & Hedges brand whose ownership is split between the British and American companies, BAT, Gallaher and Philip Morris is slightly larger at US$5,400 million.

To calculate these figures *Financial World* used a brand valuation methodology developed by the London-based marketing consultancy Interbrand. This is only one of a number of ways of valuing brands.

It begins by taking the total worldwide sales of all products sold bearing a particular brand name. So, for example, they combine all the sales of all the computers, etc. in all the world that were sold carrying the IBM name.

From this figure of total worldwide brand sales it subtracts an estimated amount which an equivalent retailer's own brand or unbranded generic product range might have generated as its operating income. These own brand estimates are calculated according to which industry the brand being analysed operated in, and so vary accordingly. IBM is compared with the computing industry expectations while Marlboro is compared with the cigarette industry. This calculation determines the *pre-tax, brand-related operating income*. Having determined the pre-tax position, two things are done.

Firstly a similar figure is calculated for the preceding year and the two figures averaged out. This removes any one year anomalies which could be caused by economic factors or short-term influences which might distort the picture of the brand's true size and strength.

Secondly it is obviously necessary to allow for taxation. For simplicity and consistency this is done by deducting tax at the maximum corporate rate in the brand-owner's home country using figures supplied by Coopers & Lybrand and Arthur Andersen, two of the world's leading accountancy firms.

This gives a figure for the *brand's net income* or, to put it more simply, *the annual amount of 'extra' money that a company*

Brand Valuation - Summary

Total world-wide brand sales

minus

equivalent own label's operating income

equals

brand related operating income

(averaged across two years.)

Maximum corporate rate tax

equals

brand's net income

Brand's net income

times

brand strength multiplier

equals

the brand's value

receives over and above what it might otherwise have expected to get if its product(s) had been unbranded.

However, this represents only one year's additional income and so it isn't a true reflection of the total value of the brand. A brand this big and successful can sensibly be expected to deliver these sorts of sums for a number of years. Therefore to estimate the long-term value of the brand, the brand's net income is factored up by a *brand strength multiplier*. This multiplier is a measure of the brand's power and is based on seven key areas which relate to the brand's strength, its ability to compete and its likely longevity.

The seven key areas determining a brand strength multiplier are as follows.

1. **Leadership**	The brand's ability to influence the market.
2. **Stability**	The proven ability of the brand to maintain a consumer franchise.
3. **Market**	The strength of the brand's trading environment.
4. **Internationality**	The ability of the brand to cross geographic and cultural borders.
5. **Trend**	The on-going direction of the brand's importance to its industry.
6. **Support**	The strength of the brand's communication.
7. **Protection**	The brand owner's legal title.

The maximum possible value of the multiplier is 20.

For service and high-tech brands there is a slight change, only a percentage of the brand's earnings, and not all the after-tax earnings are used. *Financial World* says this is because of other factors such as pricing and location in the case of airlines, restaurants and hotels, or technology innovations in the case of high-tech industries, which can be just as important as the brand name.

While Interbrand helped provide the methodology, they

are unwilling to provide any data. This is because many of the leading companies are clients of Interbrand and they want to avoid any breaches of confidentiality. They prepare their own calculations for these clients and hence their figures can vary.

The survey covered many if not most of the leading brands across a whole spectrum of industries. It is therefore possible to create league tables for different industries and identify the leading brands in each market and each category within that market. For example, in the market for drinks, the top three brands in the different categories were as follows.

BRAND	COMPANY/OWNER	BRAND VALUE 1996 US$m
Beers		
1. Budweiser	Anheuser-Busch	11,985
2. Heineken	Heineken	2,610
3. Guinness	Guinness	2,467
Spirits		
1. Johnnie Walker	Guinness	5,232
2. Bacardi	Bacardi	4,309
3. Hennessey	LVMH	2,861
Soft Drinks/Juices		
1. Coca-Cola	Coca-Cola	47,978
2. Pepsi	PepsiCo	9,320
3. Fanta	Coca-Cola	3,482
		Source: *Financial World*

Coca-Cola has in fact three of the top ten soft drinks/juices brands. As well as Coca-Cola and Fanta it owns Sprite which is at number four, worth US$2,667 million. The portfolio of these three brands alone is therefore a cool US$54,127 million!

However, beyond the, traditionally male, pre-occupation with numbers and a competitiveness to find out whose is the biggest why should people be interested in the value of brands?

Jeremy Sampson of Interbrand suggests that brand valuation can be useful for a whole variety of reasons as different people have different needs. In *Brand Valuation* he writes that brands are valued for:

♦ *Chief Executives*, wanting to unlock shareholder value, buy or sell brands as the result of changes in strategy or to increase the accountability for these valuable assets;

♦ *Bankers*, wanting to establish a fair value for brands as part of their security;

♦ *Brand Managers*, wanting to develop and extend the equity of their brands;

♦ *Advertising Agencies*, wishing to demonstrate that a reduction in ad-spend can reduce the value of the brand;

♦ *Marketing Directors*, wanting to improve the management of their brand portfolios;

♦ *Accountants*, wanting to recognise these most valuable assets on balance sheets;

♦ *Finance Directors*, establishing royalty rates for brands used by third parties in joint ventures;

♦ *Marketing Directors,* assessing the potential impact of key investment decisions such as resource allocation, disposal identification and portfolio management.

However, the key question about brand valuation that has vexed both marketers and accountants is not whether or not it should be done but rather whether or not brands should be included in the company's balance sheets. For years, marketers have referred to these assets as 'brand equity', deliberately using the financial term.

Alan Cooper in his article *Brand Equity – a lifestage model* notes:

> *Companies realise that the importance of brands extends beyond their role as marketing tools. Paul Polman of Procter & Gamble recently said that the difference between his company's market value (about US$37 billion) and the accountant's estimate of its asset*

> *value (about US$8 billion) is largely made up by the*
> *value of its brands.*

Indeed, in more recent years and amid much controversy, the idea of brand equity has been taken literally by a number of companies who proceeded to include certain brand values in their balance sheets.

In his *Handbook of Brand Management* David Arnold describes the history of what he calls the "fuss" surrounding the whole issue.

He notes that probably the first company to include a brand valuation in its balance sheet was Rupert Murdoch's Australia-based News Corporation. In 1984, News Corporation had been on an acquisition spree, buying a number of publishing titles and television licences. They had paid more for them than they had gained from them in the way of tangible assets – the machinery, plants, etc. They had been paying a premium for the brand equities of these titles and licences. They had paid extra because they believed in their ability to generate profits consistently over a period of time.

If News Corporation's balance sheet wasn't going to be severely and adversely affected they had to reflect this equity in their calculations. However, up until this time brand equity wasn't recognised as such and had always been classified as an 'intangible asset'. Traditionally these had to be written off in the year of purchase, or at best written off over a number of years as depreciated goodwill.

> *News Corporation's argument for including the*
> *premiums as an asset on the balance sheet was that the*
> *assets it had bought would produce revenue for more*
> *than one year, and so the cost should be regarded as an*
> *investment, not as a single expense item. It argued that*
> *newspaper titles and television licenses were identifiable*
> *assets, capable of producing revenue in their own right.*
> *Furthermore, they passed the acid test of 'separability',*
> *another key element in defining an asset – they could*
> *be transferred to other parties independently of the other*
> *assets of the business, 'produced' by the fixed assets of*
> *another owner, and still retain their earning power in*

*the market. By treating these titles and licenses as assets
on the balance sheet at their true current (1984) value,
they strengthened the balance sheet, increased
shareholders' funds and provided a more accurate
representation of the total assets of the company.*

In 1985, Reckitt & Colman was to be one of the first UK-quoted companies to follow suit and include brand valuations in their balance sheets, again as the result of an acquisition. After its purchase of Heublein in 1988, Grand Metropolitan included a figure of some £558 million in its balance sheet reflecting its valuation of its newly acquired Smirnoff Vodka brand.

However, these valuations continued to cause much debate, not only about the actual amounts but about the whole issue of including any figure whatsoever. The issue was further aggravated by the fact that there were different regulations on either side of the Atlantic and US companies felt disadvantaged due to the strict regulations governing any inclusion of figures in their balance sheets.

Nevertheless the crux of the matter remained the fact that valuations were always, at least in part, a subjective matter based on judgment and feelings. David Arnold concludes:

*To most informed but non-specialist observers, the
inclusion of brand valuations on balance sheets seems
something like a finance director's trick. While brands
are a real part of a company's value, their valuation
remains particularly subjective for two reasons: first,
brands are enormously complex and intangible items,
with no fixed base from which a value can be calculated;
second, there is no established market for trading
brands, as there is in property, and there are therefore
no norms in terms of valuation. Once the balance sheet
includes valuations placed on other intangibles such as
human resources, objectivity will soon disappear
altogether, rendering them useless for comparison
through time or between companies.*

One of the latest developments in this debate occurred in June 1996 when the UK Accounting Standards Board (UK

ASB) issued an exposure draft on accounting for goodwill and intangible assets. In contrast to previous papers it now appears that they support the principles that brands can be separate assets and that the value of brands need not decline over a predetermined time period, or indeed, that they need decline at all. However, how this is implemented in practice and whether the international accounting bodies will similarly change their previously sceptical points of view are yet to be seen.

What is undoubtedly true is that brands are valuable. Given the choice between the tangible and the intangible, John Stuart a former chairman of Quaker said:

> *If this business were to be split up, I would be glad to take the brands, trademarks and goodwill and you could have all the bricks and mortar and I would fare better than you.*

16

Who owns which brands?

W hat's the connection between the following brands?

They are in fact all owned by Unilever, the giant Anglo-Dutch company. As we have noted this is a company that really believes in the power of brands and is keen to get its fair share of everything we spend.

In addition, Unilever also owns:

Bird's Eye	Wall's
Oxo	Batchelors
Chicken Tonight	Colman's
Flora	Delight
Olivio	Persil
Comfort	Ragu
Radion	Timotei
Organics	Sunsilk
Cornetto	Lynx
Sure	Vaseline
Ponds	Denim
Brut	Brooke Bond
PG Tips	Red Mountain
and many more. . .	

Many of these famous brand names were originally separate companies, separate brands. Oxo and Batchelors would be just two examples. They are both now part of Van den Bergh Foods which also includes all the Brooke Bond tea brands and the margarine brands like Flora and I Can't Believe Its Not Butter. Van den Bergh Foods is itself only a division of Unilever's food business.

Now Unilever isn't alone in its penchant for multi-brand owning. Another example would be the Swiss-based Nestlé. The chart on the next page shows Nestlé's stock cupboard.

This concentration of brand ownership has many implications. The most obvious is that more of our money goes to fewer different companies than we might expect.

However, as consumers we are increasingly seeking more and more information to help guide our choices. One of the implications of this is that it is now quite possible that the actions of one specific brand can affect the prospects of many other apparently unconnected brands.

In the case of Nestlé, the action it takes to promote its baby milk brands in the Third World has had repercussions

Market	Nestlé Brands
Drinks	Nescafé, Gold Blend, Cap Colombie, Alta Rica, Perrier, Ashbourne Water, Caro, Milo, Slender, Libby's C, Um Bongo, Moonshine, Vittel, Nesquik
Confectionery	KitKat, Polo, Aero, Yorkie, Smarties, Rolo, Fruit Pastilles, Lion Bar, Toffee Crisp, After Eights, Milky Bar, Quality Street, Dairy Crunch, Walnut Whip, Toffo, Matchmakers
Dairy Products	Coffee-Mate, Tip-Top, Chambourcy, Carnation, Fussells, Ideal, Milkmaid, Nouvelle, Lyons Maid Ice Cream
Spreads & Pickles	Sun-Pat, Branston Pickle, Tartex, Pan Yan, Gales, Sarsons (vinegar), Waistline
Processed Meals/ Foods	Findus, Buitoni, Crosse & Blackwell, Maggi, Cook-in-the-Pot, Lean Cuisine
Pet Foods	Friskies, Go-Cat, Go-Dog
Cosmetics	L'Oreal
Cereals	(50 per cent ownership of Cereal Partners with Nabisco) Shredded Wheat, Shreddies, Wheatflakes, Golden Grahams, Team, Cheerio, Nesquik

on all its other brands and, in particular, its leading coffee brand, Nescafé. Baby Milk Action is a UK pressure group. It leads a 'Campaign against Nestlé', which it accuses of breaking the World Health Organisation's (WHO) guidelines on promoting its powdered milk brands.

Baby Milk Action believes that this is linked to the death

of babies in poorer developing countries. It is a fact that a baby dies every 30 seconds from unsafe bottle-feeding: breast feeding is safer. In many very poor countries, clean, safe water and the facilities to prepare hygienic bottles are few and far between. Baby Milk Action therefore opposes the promotion of baby milk brands in those countries.

One of the obstacles that Baby Milk Action faces is that even if people are aware of the issues surrounding powdered baby milk, they are unlikely to know the full extent of the Nestlé brand portfolio. Therefore they have focused their campaign on Nescafé. Wherever possible it still encourages its supporters to boycott all Nestlé products and to this end they give out a handy credit card sized list of all Nestlé's brands.

There are other reasons why a brand owner may want to distance itself from its brand. *The Independent* newspaper carried the story of one such case; the large American tobacco company, RJ Reynolds, and one of the brand they sell in Russia, Pytor I.

In Russia, following the fall of the Communist Party and the collapse of the old Soviet Union, there was an explosion of demand for Western, and in particular American, brands. People could now legally and even easily buy McDonald's hamburgers and Levi jeans, if they could afford them.

For a number of years these Western brands did exceptionally well. However, more recently there has been a resurgence in Russian nationalism, a longing for the return of a great Russian Empire. This has led to a tempering, if not an outright rejection, of some of these American brands.

The American owned company RJ Reynolds identified this trend and being a pro-active company was keen to cater to their consumers. They launched a new brand of cigarettes, Pytor I, named after Tsar Peter the Great.

> *The new brand is not subtle. The pack is jet black, decorated with a double-headed eagle, the national symbol, in which are inset the words 'Great Russia'. The blurb on the back promises to satisfy those who 'believe in the revival of the traditions and grandeur of the Russian lands'.*

> *The company's (RJ Reynolds) explanation of its strategy is simple: "Our job is to bring to the market something Russians want to buy," said André Benoit, director of external relations at the St Petersburg plant.*

From all accounts the brand is doing well.

Why then has this concentration of ownership come about? Why do companies want to own a portfolio of brands? There are two primary reasons.

The first reason is that these big multiple-brand owning companies believe in the power and value of branding. Having been successful with one brand originally they are predisposed to creating other brands. They are therefore willing to take the risks involved in launching a new brand as well as investing the large sums of money that are required nowadays.

They therefore add to their portfolio and if the new brand is successful, the company grows and they gain an even greater share of the money we spend. Organics haircare products, Impulse perfume deodorants, Ragu pasta sauces are just some of the many new brands launched by Unilever over the years.

The second reason for this concentration of brand ownership is that acquiring someone else's brands is an effective strategy open to companies seeking growth.

As we have seen, in the beginning, most brands and companies were synonymous, the Coca-Cola Company made Coca-Cola and Mars made Mars bars. Over time this evolved, the brands were line-extended (Mars King-size) and brand extended (Mars Ice-cream) as a means of supplementing organic growth.

However, many of these companies that were successful with one brand soon thought about what they might do with other brands and in particular with other people's brands.

The process of buying other brands offered them an alternative growth strategy. Whilst brands or single brand companies could grow only by organic development or brand extension, a company that acquired more brands grew by gaining these new brands' turnover and profits.

This strategy of acquiring someone else's brand is particularly appealing if you think you could do a better job with that brand than its existing brand management, or if it helps remove competition. Not surprisingly many companies nowadays have acquired large portfolios of brands and are no longer synonymous with any one brand.

In some markets this process of brand acquisition has led to a situation in which there is an intense battle between two dominant players as they go round and buy up all the competition. The toy market is a classic example.

The two 'giants' of the toy market are Hasbro and Mattel. Between them they have bought up much of their competition.

Hasbro now owns Waddingtons (Monopoly, Cluedo), Trivial Pursuit, Risk, Pictionary, Play-doh, Playskool, Sindy, Action Man, Subutteo, K-Nex and Tonka.

Mattel has a wide range of sub-brands as well as owning such names as Barbie, Fisher-Price, Tomy, Spears, Scrabble, Bluebird and Matchbox.

However, over the years these flurries of buying and selling have created interesting and sometimes strange international differences as the rights to one brand are sold to different people. In chapter fifteeen on the most valuable brands we have already noted that the Benson & Hedges brand is owned not by one company but by three: Gallaher, BAT and Philip Morris, each owning the brand in different parts of the world.

However, things can get even more complicated. As mentioned earlier, in the UK, Bird's Eye, the frozen food brand, is owned by Unilever and competes with the Nestlé-owned Findus brand. Now Unilever also sells branded frozen food across Europe, it even has a Captain to promote its fish fingers in most countries. However, the brand or rather brands are not Bird's Eye. In Germany and France that brand is Iglo and not surprisingly there is a Captain Iglo who promotes fish fingers. If that isn't awkward enough, in Italy things get more complex because there the Unilever brand is none other than Findus and yes there is a Captain Findus!

It isn't any easier in America because, while there is a frozen food brand called Bird's Eye, it's not owned by Unilever, it's owned by General Foods. In the words of an old soap opera: *"international brand ownership – confused? you will be!"*

One of the other consequences of this multiple-brand ownership is that one company can be in what, at first, could appear to be a nonsensical position, namely it appears to be competing with itself. There are many, many instances of this. The Unilever brand portfolio includes a number of margarines: Stork, Flora, Olivio and I Can't Believe Its Not Butter. Whilst to some degree these products are similar, as brands they are very different.

Stork is the most traditional brand and is closely associated with home-baking. Flora has the healthiest image and is closely associated with polyunsaturates, lowering cholesterol and heart health. I Can't Believe Its Not Butter, as its name suggests, is a great tasting alternative to butter. Olivio is based on the goodness of olive oil.

As brands they can and do appeal to different people or alternatively they may appeal to the same people but in different circumstances. For example I may use Flora on my toast and in my sandwiches in an attempt to be healthy, yet use Stork if I am baking because I know and trust its ability to help me create great results.

The Henley Centre for Forecasting observed:

> *There are often more differences between the same individual on two different occasions than between two different individuals on the same occasion.*

This basic truth, that different people have different needs and that those same people may then alter their needs at different times or in different contexts, is fundamental to the existence of brands and is also the reason that makes sense out of multiple brand owning in a single market.

17

What is brandographics?

Rory Bremner might well have been talking about brandographics rather than "women with wit" when he said the following words.

Victoria Wood can locate areas of British life and humour, very sharply and very economically, with just a brand name or two.

Brandographics is a means which can be used to segment and classify people according to what brands they buy and use. It is based on the notion that we are not just what we eat, but what we drink, what we wear, etc.

We saw earlier that we choose brands partly because they are a reflection of the sort of person we are or would like to be. Brand choice is one way in which we can express ourselves. The purchase and use of a brand not only says something about us to ourselves, it says something to everyone else as they also know and can interpret brands.

Indeed, an increasing number of observers believe that as more and more of the traditional social and cultural barriers break down it will be our role as consumers that will define who we are. What all this means is, if you can identify and understand somebody's choice of brands, it should be possible to build a picture of that person.

For example the same person could be described in the following two ways:

- He is aged between 25-34 years old. He is married and has two children. He is a white collar worker in a middle-class profession – the socio-economic class B.

- He drives a Volvo, reads *The Guardian*, shops with his wife at Sainsbury's and buys most of his suits at Next.

Which description gives you a better understanding of what this man is like?

If brandographics can provide insights like this into different people it can be used by marketers as a way of segmenting and classifying us, their consumers.

To sell their brands, marketers have to try to understand their potential customers (that's us again) or what they call their 'target audience'. They need to understand what we are like, what we want and how best to market and sell their brands to us. Brandographics is a tool they can use to market their brands more effectively. Simply by identifying and understanding what other brands we choose should give them and their agencies insights into the type of people we are and what we want.

Traditionally marketers have used demographics to help identify the particular targets for particular brands. Demographics is the study and classification of people by age, sex and marital status. It also includes the division of the population into different classes, a socio-economic classification.

People are allocated according to the occupation of the head of each household. There are six classes: A, B, C1, C2, D and E. 'A's include lawyers, doctors and company directors. They are the most respected professionals, traditionally very well paid. 'E's are the other end of the socio-economic scale, they include the unemployed and old-age pensioners.

However, if you really want to understand a specific teenager, what is more important, the job her father does or the brands of make-up she chooses to buy and wear? In more recent years, geo-demographic classifications have been developed and are increasingly used.

The most famous of these is the CACI Acorn classification. What Acorn does is divide the country up into different areas based on the different styles and types of housing and who generally lives in those types of residences. It is a classification of residential neighbourhoods.

So, for example, the Acorn type F20 is described as an "inter-war council estate, older people and accounts for 2.8 per cent of the total British population", whilst J35 is a "village with wealthy older commuters" who account for 2.9 per cent of the British population. Acorn and other geo-demographic analyses at least tell the marketer something about the type of dwelling in which his prospective consumer lives but wouldn't it be more enlightening to know what paint they use, what wallpaper they have and where they choose to go to get carpets and furniture?

So, as the traditional barriers of class and rank, council house tenant and home owner, employee and 'housewife' continue to break down, then the people who market their brands to us are likely to realise that brandographics, the study of what (other) brands you buy, may become an increasingly useful technique for them as they try to understand who we are and what we are like.

Indeed non-marketers are already using the technique even if they don't know it. In a *Vogue* article called *"Who do women really dress for?"* the journalist, Sally Brampton, describes how Jasper Conran 'segments' women.

> *Jasper Conran uses a label shorthand to define the groups women dress for. "There's the Versace woman who dresses for men, sans doubte. Versace girls make a career of sex; they don't have girlfriends, they're too much like competition. The Armani woman dresses for herself, and the Chanel woman for other women. Chanel is all about branding; you know she's a woman who wants to make other women envious."*

Branding has been described as consumer shorthand. One brand can stand for a number of specific values and meanings. A brand will have its own, and often complex, personality. Furthermore as brands are very much in the public domain and their purpose is to project their values and their personalities consistently to wide groups of people they have become powerful descriptors in their own right, standing for specific meanings.

To demonstrate this notion of brand as shorthand, imagine you are on a creative-writing course. You are asked to complete the following extract from an (imaginary) thriller by carefully selecting and inserting a limited number of words:

*"It was good to get out of the rain. I turned down the
collar on my ...... jacket.*

*'Give me a ......,' I said to the barman as I lit another
...... Looking at my ......, I realised it was a quarter after
eight and she would be here at any moment.*

*Suddenly I caught the unmistakable aroma of her ......
and there she was, looking a million dollars in that ......
dress of hers."*

It can be completed by inserting the following: brown, beer,
cigarette, watch, perfume and red, words that add some
meaning and texture to the piece. Alternatively it could read:

*"It was good to get out of the rain. I turned down the
collar on my **Armani** jacket.*

*'Give me a **Bud**,' I said to the barman as I lit another
Marlboro. Looking at my **Rolex**, I realised it was a
quarter after eight and she would be here at any moment.*

*Suddenly I caught the unmistakable aroma of her
Chanel No 5 and there she was, looking a million
dollars in that **Versace** dress of hers."*

This I would suggest builds a much fuller and richer piece,
where the reader is given more information about the people
in the piece even though roughly the same number of words
are used.

Indeed if all you then do is alter the brands you choose,
then the whole feel of the extract can change again.

*"It was good to get out of the rain. I turned down the
collar on my **C&A** jacket.*

*'Give me a **Diet Coke**,' I said to the barman as I lit
another **Lambert & Butler**. Looking at my **Timex**, I
realised it was a quarter after eight and she would be
here at any moment.*

Suddenly I caught the unmistakable aroma of her **Charlie** *and there she was, looking a million dollars in that* **Laura Ashley** *dress of hers."*

It is this ability to identify the public perception of what brands are and what they stand for that gives Victoria Wood an angle on which she can build her humour. I can just imagine her saying, "My mother-in-law is getting quite adventurous these days. Just last week she introduced my dad to Chicken Bisto."

However, as Tim Niel, a senior director with BBC Scotland says:

It's not just Victoria Wood – it's also writers like Stephen King, Bret Easton Ellis, Edith Wharton, Douglas Coupland and William Gibson who use brands as shorthand for character and have been doing so for decades.

Indeed brandographics isn't only relevant in the literary world; in the world of pop many famous stars have used the choice of brands as a key defining element.

The artist formerly known as Prince sang about a *"little red Corvette"*, Bruce Springsteen predictably sings about a Cadillac *"long and dark, shiny and black"* in his song *Cadillac Ranch* while closer to home Tom Robinson sang about the car of his dreams when he sang *"wish I had a grey Cortina, whiplash aerial, racing free"*.

Throughout this book we have seen that we can and do become very committed to certain brands. We trust them and remain loyal to them over time. We join their clubs, read their magazines and we are willing to pay and go on paying significant premiums for them. However, as brands are clearly not designed to be private we must recognise that, whether we like it or not, the commitment we show to our favourite brands says a lot about *who* we are and what we are *like*.

18

How far has branding spread?

Traditionally branding was primarily associated with products – physical things such as teas, margarines, chocolates, colas and cigarettes. Branding was about adding value to physical things. Many of the most famous brands of all time are f.m.c.g. – fast-moving-consumer-goods brands, such as Marlboro, Coca-Cola, Guinness and Levi's.

Branding theories and practices have now been applied to services such as airlines, banking, retailing and insurance with brands such as British Airways, HSBC and GAP.

Nowadays it is increasingly the case that everything is branded. It is not just products and services but people, places, pastimes and even politics that are branded.

Sports Branding

For example, Manchester United is now recognised as one of the most powerful brands in the sports world. A fact reflected not only in its ability to sell millions of replica shirts but in the way that it has been used to brand Man. United Red's Sauce in the ketchup market and Man. United premium lager in the beer market.

Like other brands, Manchester United has its loyal users and its 'non-users'. It stands for certain values in people's minds. It is uniquely positioned in its marketplace – a result partly of its size, location and history but also the values and approach it projects.

You may love Man. United or hate them but there is no denying that they are a powerful force in their marketplace. The tendency to polarise people and the fact that millions of people claim to hate them doesn't negate the fact that they are a brand. The same can be said of lots of brands – indeed there is an interesting comparison between Marmite's proud advertising claim that you either *'love it or hate it'* and the chant heard up and down the country at grounds *"Stand up if you hate Man. Utd!"*

Indeed similar to other brands, the value of Man. United far exceeds the sum of its physical assets. The combined cost of the key assets of Manchester United, the players and the ground, may be millions, even hundreds of millions of pounds, but the company now has a stock market valuation in the region of £1 billion. This difference is a reflection of the value of the Manchester United brand.

Our support for football teams also has interesting parallels with the purchasing of brands as neither is done on purely rational grounds. Blind tests (as discussed in chapter one) have regularly demonstrated that if we, the consumers, don't know or aren't told what brand we are eating or drinking we can't tell the difference between rival brands. In fact we often claim to prefer a rival's brand even though we steadfastly refuse to buy it!

So it is with football teams. Your team can regularly lose and clearly not be the most successful team in the country, yet it is still your team. Objectively your team may not play better or more enjoyable football but even that doesn't stop it being your team. If all there was to football was winning or being the best, then no one would support teams from the lower divisions.

Spice Girls – Brand Power

The pop world is another sector that seems to have taken branding to heart. The Spice Girls are a textbook example of some of the latest approaches to branding, namely where branding is recognised to start with a set of values and a persona which can then be applied to a range of different products and/or services. (An approach to branding that is described more fully in chapter twenty.)

The Spice Girls stand for a unique set of values and a persona that they sum up as 'Girl Power'. This is the core concept of their brand. These values could be applied to a whole range of products and services. Pop music was, however, the obvious and appropriate first choice. Hear, sing and dance to Girl Power! – then buy the CD or cassette and come to the concert.

Like other successful brands, this brand has extended in other markets based on the same set of values. It has stretched to numerous other markets ranging from cinema, *Spice Girls – The Movie*, come and see Girl Power in action, to body deodorants, "Impulse Spice – men can't help acting on Girl Power!". The Spice Girls are truly a rubber b(r)and!

Interestingly the Spice Girls are also a textbook example of another aspect of branding – brand architecture (see chapter three). The individual Spice Girls are examples of endorsed sub-brands.

Each of the different girls – four or five depending on whether this is WG or PG (with Geri or post Geri) are a sub-brand in their own right. They remain true to, and are an expression of, Girl Power but also bring their own dimension or twist to that concept. They add distinctive values and personalities of their own which are consistent with the core notion of Girl Power, but which are also building on it.

Do you want Scary Spice Girl Power or Baby Spice Girl Power?

Using Tango as a parallel, there is a core concept of distinctive, quirky, in your face, British soft drinks and also a range of sub-brands that not only offer different flavours but different benefits and personalities too.

Do you want seductive, British, in your face Apple Tango or the explosive hit of British, in your face Orange Tango?

New Labour, New Branding

New Labour is another example of a brand approach being adopted in a non-traditional area. Even the name is a give-away: *"New Labour - now with added Tony"*.

In fact, the success of new Labour is a great case history for aspiring brand managers, especially those faced with an ageing and lack-lustre brand. Looking at what the party did, it is possible to draw parallels with much of the best of brand management.

New Labour's resurgence started with a frank appraisal of where the brand was, its strengths and weaknesses and an understanding of how its consumers, the voters, had changed. Many of the established brand planning processes, the 'planning cycles', start by asking "Where are we?" and

"Why are we here?"

Then, in the light of this learning, Labour recognised that the traditional expression of its core values and the way it presented itself was unlikely to gain it the 'sales' – votes – it needed.

Rather than changing those values, which would have effectively undermined the reason for the brand itself, it chose to try to find ways in which to express those values in a way that was relevant and appealing today.

This approach has direct parallels with that recommended by Collins and Porras in their book *Built to Last*. They examined eighteen visionary brands and compared each with one of their closest rivals to discover what made these brands so exceptional.

Whilst Collins and Porras suggest a full framework, for them the central concept is expressed as:

Preserve the core, stimulate progress.

They convincingly argue that this is not a contradiction – '*A tyranny of the OR*' but a '*Genius of the AND*'. In other words it's not a case of either/or but of both/and. You need to remain true to core values whilst evolving other elements of what you do as necessary.

> *It is absolutely essential not to confuse core ideology with culture, strategy, tactics, operations, policies, or other noncore practices. Over time, cultural norms must change; strategy must change; product lines must change; goals must change; competencies must change; administrative policies must change; organization structure must change; reward systems must change. Ultimately, the only thing a company should not change over time is its core ideology – that is, if it wants to be a visionary company.*

In the run up to the 1997 election and in the face of increasing provocation from the Conservatives that they lacked specific policies, New Labour continued to promote and push its values instead. They felt that it was more important to establish their positioning, their values and beliefs in the minds of the voters rather than any specific policy.

As discussed earlier in this book, branding is about more than a specific product or service, these can and do change; branding is about values and attributes. Labour recognised the need to re-establish these before moving on to the 'products or services' – the policies.

Here there is an interesting parallel with the financial industry. This is a market where the leading companies have generally been around for considerable periods of time but whose brands are relatively undeveloped. One of the key reasons for this is the fact that it's an industry that has focused on promoting its products, its accounts and their features, the interest rates, and not their values and personalities. This was also why the market was vulnerable, not only to the entry of value-based offers from the multiple retailers such as Tesco and Sainsbury, but also to the arrival of more fully developed brands such as Virgin.

However, that is not to say that values are enough in their own right. As Tony Blair has said:

> *I believe in the values that gave birth to this party but I have always believed that values without practical implementation is just so much idle dreaming. Idle dreaming doesn't mean anything.*

Numerous brand theorists have likened the brand to a promise from a supplier to the consumer. More important is that it's a promise *that must be kept*. It's not just a promise; it's a responsibility.

So when, in the final fun up to the election, the Labour party decided to announce its key policies and targets by which it wanted to be judged, it is perhaps not so surprising that these were announced as pledges.

Finally, much has been made of the supposed tight control of Labour's central office on Millbank and the role of the army of spin-doctors, but again there are parallels with brand management. In brand management there are strict quality controls on production lines, clear principles for the behaviour of service staff and the power wielded by brand and advertising managers in selecting how and where the brands present themselves to their consumers.

Disney's control over its staff and the strict discipline it maintains is legendary and is one of the reasons why it is so successful as a brand.

Location Branding

It is often said that branding a service is more difficult than branding a product. Whilst not easy, at least with product brands mass production techniques offer an element of consistency in a way that is hard to mirror in a service business.

Services are 'people businesses' which rely on the interaction of employees and us, their customers, as well as the functioning of the business itself.

Taking British Airways as an example, and thinking about just one journey, there are a huge number of contact points which determine our perception of the brand.

There are the mechanics of flying which include the plane, how it is outfitted, the food served and the films shown, the lounge, how it is outfitted and stocked. These are the equivalent of a product brand's product. However, in addition there are all those points where customers and BA employees interact and they all can affect the perception of the brand.

There is the representative on the BA sales desk, the greeter who directs you to the right area of the airport, the check-in assistant, the staff in the executive lounge, the cabin crew, the captain and flight staff. At all these points there is the opportunity to make a positive impression for the brand but equally it is possible to make a negative impression. One employee who has had a bad day or is in a bad mood has the potential to undo all the good work done by the rest of the organisation.

If that isn't difficult enough, imagine the complexities of trying to brand a country or region. Again there is a product – the place itself, its natural and man-made resources, but the 'employees', those people who will interact with potential customers, not only number in millions but they are not 'employees'. They have no incentive to act as the brand owner wants.

This leads to a further complexity – who is it that owns and manages the brand? In fact who the 'brand manager' is depends on which element of location branding is being considered.

Generally there are two types of location branding: destination and development branding. Destination branding is branding a location as a desirable location for visiting. Its aim is to increase tourism.

Economic development is branding an area as a desirable place in which to set up, run or invest in a business. Its aim is to increase investment and employment in the area.

In most destination branding, the brand manager is the relevant tourist board or council whose remit is to act on behalf of the tourist industry of that area.

Springpoint, brand and corporate identity consultants, has worked on a number of destination branding projects and their chief executive, Fiona Gilmore, has highlighted some of the particular difficulties:

> *Brand positioning for a location can be a difficult task because there are so many uncontrollable elements and so many possible points of contact. That is why the brand has to be an amplification and not a fabrication. The idea should be aspirational and something that really makes a difference. Only then will you get the people inside onside.*
>
> *There can also be a need to balance stereotypical perceptions of a country that local people can find patronising or misrepresentative with what is actually attractive to potential visitors.*

> *While it is true that it rains in Wales and there are a lot of sheep, there is so much more to Wales and the Welsh people. It's a land of legend and nature with a spirit of*

'Hwyl' – a Welsh word for the pride and passion that a Welshman feels for his homeland.

Branding is truly a phenomenon: it has become almost a necessity in the modern world where products, services, pastimes, politics and pop are all branded. However, it doesn't stop there ... think about schools, universities and even yourself. How are you branded?

19

Is branding on the web really that different to other forms of branding?

Is mass marketing due for a cataclysmic shakeout? Absolutely. A new form of marketing is changing the landscape, and it will affect Interruption Marketing as significantly as the automobile affected the makers of buggy whips.

So says Seth Godin in *Permission Marketing,* as he argues that traditional mass marketing, based on advertising that 'interrupts' us, is about to undergo a fundamental change.

He draws an analogy with two strategies for getting married:

The Interruption Marketer buys an extremely expensive suit. New shoes. Fashionable accessories. Then, working with the best database and marketing strategists, selects the demographically ideal singles bar.

Walking into the singles bar, the Interruption Marketer marches up to the nearest person and proposes marriage. If turned down, the Interruption Marketer repeats this process on every person in the bar.

If the Interruption Marketer comes up empty-handed after spending the entire evening proposing, it is obvious that the blame should be placed on the suit and the shoes. The tailor is fired. The strategy expert who picked the bar is fired. And the Interruption Manager tries again at a different singles bar.

If this sounds familiar, it should. It's the way most large marketers look at the world. They hire an agency. They build fancy ads. They 'research' the ideal place to run the ads. They interrupt people and hope that one in a hundred will go ahead and buy something. Then, when they fail, they fire their agency!

The other way to get married is a lot more fun, a lot more rational, and a lot more successful. It's called dating.

A Permission Marketer goes on a date. And then another. Until, after ten or twelve dates, both sides can really communicate with each other about their needs and desires. After twenty dates they meet each other's families. Finally after three or four months of dating, the Permission Manager proposes marriage.

Permission Marketing is just like dating. It turns strangers into friends and friends into lifetime customers. Many of the rules of dating apply, and so do many of the benefits.

Godin's argument is that in today's world we only have a set amount of time, there is only a set amount of money and therefore the more products that are offered on the market the less money there is to go around.

What this means is that 'Interruption Marketers', as Godin calls traditional marketers, have to increase their spending on advertising if they want to capture our attention. However, as more and more is spent on advertising, it not only costs the marketers more but also increases the amount of clutter, so making any communication more difficult.

It is a classic 'Catch 22': the more they spend the less effective it is; the less effective it is, the more they spend.

Godin's answer is 'Permission Marketing'. This is based on providing an incentive to volunteers and then building a relationship that is anticipated, personal and relevant. Godin says it isn't a new concept but one that new technology and the internet in particular allow to be practised much more effectively. He goes on to suggest that this new approach to marketing will have a *'cataclysmic'* effect.

Godin is just one of many who argue that new technology is changing the face of marketing.

At *Cluetrain.com,* Levine, Locke, Searls and Weinberger argue even more strongly that:

> *A powerful global conversation has begun. Through the Internet, people are discovering and inventing new ways to share relevant knowledge with blinding speed. As a direct result, markets are getting smarter – getting smarter faster than most companies.*
>
> *These markets are conversations. Their members communicate in language that is direct, funny and often shocking. Whether explaining or complaining, joking or serious, the human voice is unmistakably genuine. It can't be faked.*
>
> *Most corporations, on the other hand, only know how to talk in the soothing, humourless monotone of the mission statement, marketing brochure and your-call-is-important-to-us busy signal. Same old tone, same old lies. No wonder networked markets have no respect for companies unable or unwilling to speak as they do.*
>
> *But learning to speak in a human voice is not some trick, nor will corporations convince us they are human with lip service about 'listening to customers'. They will only sound human when they empower real human beings to speak on their behalf.*
>
> *While many such people already work for companies today, most companies ignore their ability to deliver genuine knowledge, opting instead to crank out sterile happytalk that insults the intelligence of markets literally too smart to buy it.*
>
> *However employees are getting hyperlinked even as markets are. Companies need to listen carefully to both. Mostly, they need to get out of the way so intra-networked employees can converse directly with internetworked markets.*

> *Corporate firewalls have kept smart employees in and*
> *smart markets out. It's going to cause real pain to tear*
> *those walls down. But the result will be a new kind of*
> *conversation. And it will be the most exciting*
> *conversation business has ever engaged in.*

As discussed earlier in this book, branding is over 2,000 years old and while the concept has evolved over that time, it is true to say that it hasn't changed as much as many other aspects of commerce. Even without the digital revolution the business world has seen a fundamental change in the last 250 years with the industrial revolution, the internal combustion engine, electricity, mass production, the computer, telephone and mobile phone, radio, cinema, TV and video. The list goes on...

As the pace of change has quickened, people have argued that we have moved into a new technological age and are in the midst of an e-revolution.

Some have gone on to argue that the traditional concepts of a brand and brand positioning are outmoded, that they are too stationary. Brands need to evolve and adapt at the pace of life, not at the pace of marketing departments. As Levine *et al.* say, there is a belief that brands need to be more fluid, more personal, if they are to manage the more direct relationships that digital media allow.

Some strong web based brands are emerging, with 'Amazon' and 'Yahoo!' as two obvious examples. Both of these have used the amazing capabilities of the internet to great effect, to engage their customers in conversations.

Like many other internet retailers, Amazon is able to compete on the basis of range and price. The advantages of not having to run and staff expensive retail outlets and to be able to source books and then send them out mean that it, like many other internet booksellers, can offer a stock of more than 1.5 million books, many of which are discounted.

However, it isn't just this that made Amazon such a success. If it wasn't a first mover in the market, it certainly was an early mover. This undoubtedly helped but it wasn't the only reason for success.

Amazon offered innovative benefits and services. The opportunity to write your own review of a book and have it published played to the strengths of the media and the desires of their target audience. Many book readers would love to write and have something – anything, published: here was their chance. Thousands took it. Book buyers also welcomed the chance to read what other 'real' people had to say about the books in real *'human voices'* not marketing speak, an idea that is strongly advocated in *The Cluetrain Manifesto.*

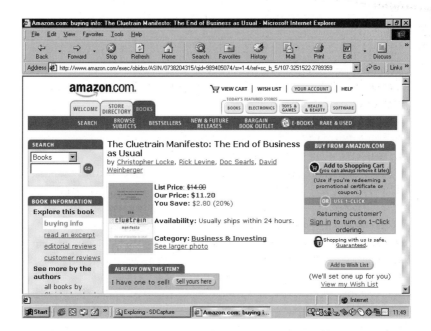

The personalised welcome back messages and Amazon's lists of other books they think you might like come across as friendly suggestions, not a heavy sell. So too do the details of what other books the last person to buy the book you are considering bought.

The brand seems to really understand its target audience and has a real interest in books. It engages and interacts with its customers on what appears to be an individual level.

It also works hard on ensuring rapid and prompt delivery, keeping you informed by e-mail along the way. This commitment to efficient delivery again marks it out from other retailers on the net. It has recognised that while a brand is a promise it is a promise that must be kept and has therefore been willing to invest millions to ensure it fulfils its responsibilities.

Yahoo! has also been a success story, establishing itself as the most popular site on the web.

From its name, its tagline – '*Do you Yahoo?*', its design, its advertising, its ease of navigation and its ability to let you personalise your interaction with 'My Yahoo!', the brand has consistently built a distinctive offer and personality.

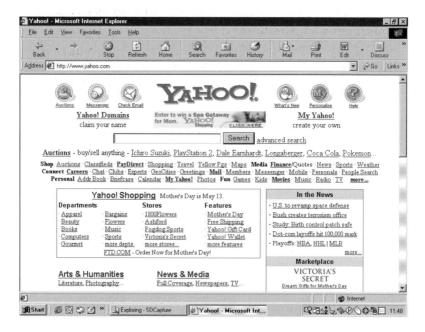

Yahoo! has therefore been able to build relationships rapidly with its customers using the power and technology of the web to create levels of personalised interaction that are far greater than many traditional brands. Yahoo! has been an exponent of permission marketing, building its relationships by gaining the permission of its users and slowly building them over time.

Despite some obvious differences about the level of personalisation, the levels of interaction and the speed of development, both Amazon and Yahoo! conform to many of the 'traditional' definitions of what a brand is:

♦ They both represent a set of values and attributes

applied to, in their cases, a service. They offer both functional and emotional benefits.

♦ They have developed distinct brand personalities.

♦ They represent a promise to their customers and understand that to be successful they must keep their promises.

♦ Like brands in other markets they also face ever-increasing levels of competition so have needed a clear positioning to differentiate themselves.

In *Differentiate or Die*, Jack Trout and Steve Rivkin examine health web sites, highlighting the number of them and how they differentiate themselves:

> *Consider one of the most popular of the cybercrazes, web sites devoted to health or maladies. The target market is a big one: cyber-chondriacs. Already we have the following sites and their pitches...*

> **Medscan Inc.** *Get your medical information from the site that doctors use.*
> *medscape.com*

> **WebMD Inc**. *Come for the content, stay for the 'community'.*
> *webmd.com*

> **Drkroop.com Inc**. *Trust Dr. Kroop.*
> *drkroop.com*

> **American's Health Network**. *Surgery happens, and you are there!*
> *ahn.com*

> **Mediconsult.com Inc**. *Information for patients and those who care for them.*
> *mediconsult.com*

> **InteliHealth Inc**. *Information vetted by John Hopkins*

doctors, presented with flair.
intelihealth.com

AmericasDoctor.com Inc. *A doctor is always in.*
Americasdoctor.com

ThriveOnline. *Wellness and the 'new health'.*
Thriveonline.com

On Health Network Co. *The holistic health site.*
onhealth.com

Again this is not any different from the situation facing almost all the traditional brands in their markets. Take the shampoo market, for example, the competition includes:

♦ **Timotei** – Healthy hair naturally

♦ **Pantene** – Specially formulated (with ingredients such as Pro-Vitamin B) to give you beautiful, healthy hair

♦ **Head & Shoulders** – Effective dandruff control

♦ **Wash&Go** – Beautiful hair conveniently

♦ **Clairol's Herbal Essence** – The pleasurable way to create beautiful, desirable hair

♦ **Johnson's Baby Shampoo** – Gentle enough for babies of all ages

♦ **Organics** – Energy from the root

♦ **Fructis** – With active fruit concentrates

♦ **L'Oreal Elvive** – Clinically proven results, because you're worth it

Additionally, not all brands on the web are internet brands; many are the web manifestation of existing brands. Indeed in 2000 the largest e-retailer in the UK was not an internet brand. It was in fact Tesco.

So it would seem that whilst the internet was billed as revolutionary when it comes to branding, it is perhaps fairer to say that it has been evolutionary. It is encouraging change but many of the underlying principles of branding apply equally well to traditional brands as they do to internet brands.

One final thought on the similarity of traditional branding and internet branding comes courtesy of Julie Meyers, founder member of *First Tuesday*, the 'blind-dating' service that helped launch many of the dotcom brands. She has coined the phrase the '*90% Club*' for the 90 per cent of dotcom companies she feels will go to the wall. Brands like Boo, Wowgo and Clickmango that came, spent and went are members of the club.

What hasn't been commented on, however, is the striking similarity that 90 per cent has to '9 out of 10', which as traditional brand marketers all know is the supposed failure rate for new brands.

So perhaps things haven't changed that much after all.

20

What does the future hold for branding?

The end of branding has been predicted with surprising regularity. April 21st 1993 is known as 'Black Friday'. On that day, the giant Philip Morris company announced its plans to slash the price of its most famous and valuable brand – Marlboro.

Many analysts immediately heralded it as the beginning of the end for brands. If a brand like Marlboro could not support its price premium – the *raison d'être* for a brand as far as the City is concerned – then what were the chances for other lesser brands.

Articles with titles such as *"The brand is dead"* appeared on both sides of the Atlantic and share prices of many leading brand companies fell, wiping millions of pounds of value from these companies. But like many such stories, the truth was a little different.

Marlboro had indeed been losing market share to other brands and retailers' own label equivalents, and the main reason was price. Marlboro was significantly more expensive than these competitors. While it is true that a strong brand is supposed to support, indeed justify, a price premium, in the case of Marlboro in the early 1990s the premium had been steadily increasing.

The Marlboro brand is owned by Philip Morris and at that time it was trying to recoup some of the costs of a recent take over. It had therefore been steadily increasing the premium being charged. It wanted to increase its profits from Marlboro. Now brands, even the most famous ones, have their limits and Philip Morris had pushed Marlboro too far.

Without knowing this background the price cut would indeed appear a significant chink in the brand's armour, but viewed in this context it can be seen as a re-balancing of the situation. The brand has since regained share and still charges, indeed has always charged, a premium over other products. As we saw in chapter fifteen, it is still regarded as the second most valuable brand in the world.

The brand is dead; long live the brand!

On the other hand, taking a longer-term view, there is truth in the notion that traditional manufacturer brands are indeed on the wane. The growth of own label products is a clear demonstration of this fact. In many of the traditional consumer goods markets, such as food and drink, the share of the market controlled by manufacturers has declined significantly over the last twenty years.

Even this doesn't mean an end to branding. Rather it is an evolution of branding. 'Own label', as it is often called, isn't unbranded – it's just not branded by the manufacturer.

The products, produced by a wide variety of companies and organisations, are not separate product brands but are the product offering of a retail brand. We don't buy unbranded yoghurts, cereals, toilet paper or wine; we buy Tesco's yoghurts, Tesco's cereals, Tesco's toilet paper and Tesco's wine or indeed the other supermarket equivalents.

Retailers have increasingly become the big, dominant brands in many of today's marketplaces and they have extended their brands into an increasing number of areas including petrol and financial services.

Some observers believe that in the longer term new forms of branding may take this separation of manufacturer and retailer even further. In March 1996, one of the industry's leading journals, *Marketing,* ran a leader entitled *"Brand owning in the 21st Century"* where it proposed Virgin as an example of such a brand.

> *What it has is purity. Virgin expresses an idea, unsullied by any grubby connotations of product or sector. It can be, and has been, applied to anything that 'feels' right, be it a cola or personal equity plan, and consumers understand that all the values that apply to one product – good service, style, quality, value and fair dealing – apply to all the others.*
>
> *It is an intangible that is worth millions to its owner, and now we're starting to see the real payback. After*

the huge success of Peps comes health insurance, life assurance and pensions. Frankly the existing players aren't going to know what's hit them. Bupa and PPP are brands in name only, the latter's re-launch notwithstanding. It would be difficult for a typical consumer to express how one differs from the other, except perhaps in price. The same goes for most pension funds.

Virgin may be a frothy newcomer, but we do know what it stands for, because Richard (Branson) has told us – no jargon, no middlemen, no commission, no salesmen and no hidden charges. Virgin's products are rarely ground-breaking. The Peps on offer are from Norwich Union, for example. What gives it an edge is classic marketing. It found out what the customer wants and is supplying it at a price he (or she) can afford.

Virgin is a 21st century company, with a 21st century brand. In its operation of brand ownership it takes the *retailer own-label idea one step further. If Sainsbury can put its name to products made by others, why is there any longer a need for manufacturers to own brands?*

Does Procter & Gamble need to actually make soap powder, or Mazda bolt cars together?

This approach literally stands the traditional model of branding on its head.

The orthodoxy is that you create a brand by starting with a product to which you add values and attributes through naming, packaging and advertising, and over time a brand is established in the mind of the consumer.

This 21st century approach is that you start with the brand, its values and attributes – a defined set of principles – which are then consistently applied to products and services that are appropriate. In other words where they 'feel right'.

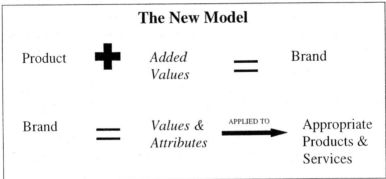

The Traditional Model

Product + Added Values = Brand

The New Model

Product **+** *Added Values* **=** Brand

Brand **=** *Values & Attributes* APPLIED TO → Appropriate Products & Services

As the *Marketing* leader concluded:

Maybe it's time we accepted the obvious – that you don't need to make it to sell it.

Whether making or just selling them, brands have more recently become a target for many commentators who are now predicting a global backlash – and perhaps even another end to branding!

Naomi Klein has topped the business book best sellers' list with *No logo*. In it she points an accusing finger at what she sees as the unsavoury dominance of big brands and predicts a *'brand boomerang'*. Interviewed in *The Observer* she described her book as:

> *...a story about the loss of public space and steady jobs, about restricting public choice and most of all about expanding corporate power. It is a story about what lies behind the brand and the people standing up to the brand bullies.*

She feels that:

> *A mania has gripped the world. It's called branding. It's not advertising, it's about building a spiritual mythology around corporations.*

In some countries some people seem to be taking her book title *No Logo* as a call to action. There is a trend for 'de-logo-ing'. This involves the physical removal of any logo on particular goods – cutting holes in your brand new Nike t-shirt to remove the swoosh, removing the red tab from your Levi's. It is seen as a statement that you are rejecting the commercially accepted norms of the world.

Klein recently told an audience of protesters in Prague that global capitalism was giving kids *"Pepsi instead of blood and Microsoft Windows instead of brains"*.

It seems that she is not alone in feeling this way.

With the Cold War effectively over, the 'baddies' in pictures are increasingly portrayed as corporations or big brands. In the James Bond movie *The World is not Enough* the baddie is an evil media tycoon who is trying to engineer a world crisis as a means to more effectively launch his brand – a new TV news station.

In *Austin Powers – The Spy who Shagged me*, the arch baddie's headquarters are deliberately and perhaps pointedly situated beneath a Starbucks, a brand that at the time was under attack in the American press as exploitative.

Websites such as Cluetrain.com, mentioned in chapter nineteen, rail against the corporate marketing speak of modern brands

A Canadian based magazine *Adbusters* promotes what is being called 'culture jamming'. Its founder Kalle Lasn writes in his book *Culture Jam: The Uncooling of America*:

> *Corporations advertise and culture jammers subvertise.*

The organisation has produced a series of striking images *'subvertising'* classic advertising campaigns of many big brands.

Tommy Hilfiger's all-American campaign is parodied in an 'ad' that has the stars and stripes as a backdrop. However, instead of the beautiful all-American kids there is a herd of sheep and the line *"Tommy – follow the herd"*.

Another ad parodies the Calvin Klein after-shave and perfume campaigns. A beautifully shot, black and white picture of a very hairy pot-bellied male torso is entitled *"Reality"*.

Consumer activism is clearly increasing, whether this is Babymilk Action, as discussed in chapter sixteen, the 'Buy Nothing Day' promoted by *Adbusters*, the Shell boycott led by Greenpeace or the anti-capitalism demonstrations timed to coincide with meetings of the G7 group of countries.

But is this really the end of brands?

Unlikely. As has been argued throughout this book, branding is one of the biggest cultural phenomena of the last century and in one respect Naomi Klein is correct: branding is increasingly all-pervasive. As we have seen, branding is now everywhere and everything is branded from products to pop stars, from services to sports, from corporations to countries.

Having said that, branding is unlikely to remain unaffected. Specific brands may well be hit and hit badly, especially if they aren't seen to be listening and responding. And in a world where there is more and more information available brands are going to need to be more transparent about their beliefs and their processes. The old adage of *legal, decent, honest and truthful* is a sensible rallying cry.

A number of brands are taking this further and are actively ensuring that they are seen to be putting something back into the community and/or adopting high profile campaigns supporting charities.

Hence you have Tesco's regular and highly successful Computers for Schools promotion, Unilever's (and Birds Eye's) establishment of the Marine Stewardship Council with the WWF (WorldWide Fund for Nature not the World Wrestling Federation!) and Daddies teaming up with the NSPCC to donate part of the proceeds of every sale to the cause. Many brands are now openly talking about a second bottom line – the social one.

There is a brand of confectionery in the states called 'Fifty-fifty' where fifty percent of all the profits are donated to charity and The Body Shop has long espoused this approach.

Another trend emerging in branding is a move towards the 'corporate brand'. As Robert Dwek noted in an article in the advertising industry's top journal, *Campaign*:

> *Change is in the air because the corporate branding philosophy is gaining global dominance. So companies like Virgin – to borrow an analyst's phrase, 'top down' companies – are in the ascendant, and 'bottom up' companies (those that associate brands with individual products) are very much out in the cold.*

He highlighted the fact that the Western world's definition of brands has traditionally been closely associated with specific products whereas in Japan and other Eastern economies broad-based corporate brands are much more the norm:

> *Mitsubushi, for example, manufactures products ranging from cars to stereos, and from medical equipment to textiles, as well as being in the shipbuilding and banking industries. Sony makes Michael Jackson records as well as pocket calculators. The same applies to other Far Eastern titans like Samsung, Hyundai and Yamaha.*

Why is this happening?

Well, as we have seen, the cost of creating and building a brand, which was always high, has risen even more. In particular the cost of advertising has risen exponentially since the introduction of television advertising.

A broad-based corporate brand can help facilitate the launch of new products or sub-brands. These new entrants are given a running start because they are endorsed by their well-known, hopefully well-respected and ideally well-loved parent brand.

Consumers may not know what the new product or sub-brand is but they know the parent brand and what its values and personality are. They are therefore more willing to try this new entrant based on their previous experience of, and their goodwill towards, the parent brand.

Advertising at a corporate brand level can also offer economies of scale. Advertising can be used to promote the corporate brand and its values, attributes and personality that can then have what is known as a 'halo' effect on its entire range of products. In other words it creates a positive image under which the brand's products and services can bask. This is obviously much cheaper than advertising each product and service separately.

Again a retailer such as Tesco is a good example of this. Tesco is now one of the UK's largest advertisers. It doesn't advertise all the different products it sells under its brand name, rather it tends to advertise specific features of its stores and their services, such as its 'one in front policy' of opening more tills if any queue has more than two people in it. In fact, given the breadth of its product range there is no way Tesco could economically afford to advertise each separate product.

Already there is a trend that has seen us, as consumers, demanding more and more information about the brands we buy. We are learning that one corporate brand can own many different brands (see chapter sixteen). What's more we not only want to know who makes the brands we choose but what their values are and perhaps more importantly who to complain to and who to take issue with if the need arises. This in effect forces the corporate brands to reveal themselves.

Another reason has been the increasing recognition of the

importance of branding by the City. Companies are much more valuable than the sum of their tangible assets, and their intangible assets include not only the specific brands any company owns but the corporate brand itself.

The image and reputation of the company may play a role with the consumer by helping persuade us to buy the company's products and services but it can have other corporate benefits too. A strong corporate brand can be vital in the recruitment of the best graduates, in helping to retain the most valuable people and perhaps most importantly it can make the final difference when it comes to a company's ability to raise funds on the stock market or other means of investment.

In addition the popularity of branding with consumers, the City and marketing departments has also led some companies to adopt the language of branding for the first time; for example the big accountancy and law firms. It is perfectly reasonable to argue that in building their often highly successful businesses they created a vision, a set of values and a unique culture, key elements of what many would define as a corporate brand. Until recently, however, they have neither marketed themselves on this basis nor ensured everyone with the company bought into these ideas fully.

The growth of corporate brands is therefore also a result of new sectors of different industries adopting a more overtly brand-led approach.

What else does the future hold for branding?

Brands will increasingly need to be based on distinctive values and personalities as the never-ending improvements in technology will mean competitors will 'me-too' any new products more quickly and more easily than ever before. Even where a brand can create a discernible point of difference, the window it will have to exploit that position will get shorter and shorter.

Take for example the much-publicised launch of British Airways revolutionary bed-chair – the first fully reclining seat. Singapore Airways launched their version six months later and within a year Virgin offered the double bed version amid many jokes about the mile high club.

The 'new model' for brands described earlier in the chapter, which starts with values and personality and then applies them to whatever products or services are appropriate, will increasingly become the norm. The core of a brand's positioning will be defined less by its original product or market and more by a vision and set of values. The result will be a more adaptable, broader based and long-term basis for defining a brand.

As a result there will be more broad-based brands, many of which will be corporate brands. They will offer a wide range of products and services. The continuing increasing cost of developing and building any new brands will mean that most new brands will be created, not on the basis of a single product but on the premise of a range of products and services.

Economies of scale and the 'shrinking' of the world that has come with improved technology, transportation and communication will mean that these new brands will be created to be international, even global. The old custom of developing a brand for a specific country, then rolling it out across the world if successful, will be the exception not the rule.

This won't be the only reason why there may be fewer brands. A number of the traditional manufacturers have announced plans to focus on a smaller number of what they hope will be bigger brands. Unilever is leading the way, having announced plans to cut its list of 1600 brands to 600 brands.

There will be fewer product(s)-only brands. The need to control their own distribution and destiny, the need to have direct contact with us, their ever more demanding consumer will drive brands to create service or retail versions of themselves. They will want to know each and every one of us, and our particular needs, better if they do not want to lose our custom to a competitor.

Indeed many of the existing 'traditional' brands have already identified this need and have moved into retail and/ or service industries to augment their offers.

Consider NikeTown sports shops, Legoland theme parks, Nescafé cafés, Levi clothing stores, Häagen Dazs ice cream parlours, Covent Garden Soups kiosks, Disney shops, CadburyWorld Visitor Centre, The Clarins studios, Amoy noodle bars and the Lynx barber shops. The list is increasing almost daily as brands that in the past made only products are realising that brands exist in the minds of consumers and that we can be tempted and encouraged to experience our brands in a multitude of ways.

As Pine and Gilmore say in their book, *The Experience Economy*:

> *Goods and services are no longer enough, brands need to create experiences that engage customers in an inherently personal way.*

The digital age is also allowing brands, both new and established, to create new ways of interacting with their customers.

We, their customers, are willing, even eager, to demonstrate our loyalties and commitment to our favourite brands because they offer us the means to express ourselves, our values and our dreams. They connect us in brand clans, in brand clubs.

The brands of the future will be much less reliant on television advertising and the 30-second commercial. Niall

Fitzgerald, the Chairman of Unilever, made no apologies when he highlighted this in an address to the European Association of Advertising Agencies in Dublin:

> *There are vast and irreversible changes taking place in the world of communications; and not one of those changes will favour network television ... digitisation, the new technology, the convergence of computing and telecommunications services, the plunging unit costs of equipment, rising levels of disposable income and the de-regulation of the airwaves all mean that simple one-way communication has its best and biggest days behind it.*

The brands of tomorrow will want to engage in a dialogue with us, their customers. They are now aware that communication is a two-way process. It's about listening as well as talking. One to one marketing, permission marketing, will become more and more important. If in the past most brand communication was about 'broad' casting, the future will see more 'narrow' casting.

So while a few argue that we are heading for a major brand backlash, it is hard to really envisage a future where brands don't exist. The fall of the Soviet Union and the first suggestions of a creeping commercialisation of China make it all the more difficult to do so. Brands are so much part of society, so intrinsic to so many businesses and as a concept so adaptable, they appear to be here to stay.

Branding has been one of the cultural phenomena of the 20th century and it seems likely that the same will be true in the 21st century. Brands and branding won't stand still; they will continue to evolve. If anything they will get more, not less, important because, to paraphrase the quotation from Charles Revlon at the beginning of the book, while we increasingly recognise that they are only cosmetics we would still rather buy a brand that offers us hope!

The brand glossary – what do the different terms with the word 'brand' in them actually mean?

brand A set of specific values and attributes represented by a name, a symbol or some combination of both and applied to a product or service or range of products and services.

brandographics The definition and segmentation of people by their usage of brands.

brand architecture The hierarchy of branding as it is applied to a specific product or service. How a company structures its use of different levels and types of branding. Most often this is demonstrated by the use of parent brand and sub-brand.

brand clans Groups of people who are so committed to a specific brand that they are akin to unpaid advocates for that brand.

brand equity The level of goodwill that has been engendered by a brand. In many ways the most valuable aspects of any brand.

brand extension The use of an existing brand name on a new product or service entering a market or market sector that is different from the original market of that brand.

brand icons The symbols and images intrinsically linked with a brand. They may represent the brand name, an attribute of the brand or the brand's personality.

brand leader   The brand with the largest share of a specific market. It is theoretically possible to have two brand leaders in the same market as one can be the brand leader in value terms whilst a different brand is larger in volume terms.

brand lifecycle   The ability of a brand to extend its lifetime beyond the life of any one of the products and services it offers.

brand loyalty   The level of commitment consumers demonstrate for a particular brand.

brand manager   An executive who has responsibility for the management of a brand. Nowadays the executive who has the title is the actual title is only a junior member of a broader brand management team and is no longer the 'managing director' of a brand as the title was originally described by Procter & Gamble.

brand management The process of looking after a brand. It is often simplified as the four Ps: product, price, place and promotion.

brand name   The legal word used to designate the product and services of a particular brand. They truly range from the sublime to the ridiculous.

brand personality The characteristics of a brand described in humanistic terms which while it sounds difficult to do is surprisingly easy for well defined brands.

brand positioning How a brand is located in its market and placed relative to its competition. It is a summation of what the brand offers the consumers and what differentiates it from the competition. It comprises four elements: the target group, the frame of reference, the brand offer and how that offer is differentiated versus the competition.

brand repostioning The relocation of a brand in the consumers' mind achieved by altering one of the four elements of a brand positioning.

brand strength multiplier A figure between 0 and 20 used by *Financial World* in the calculation of a brand's value. It is the figure by which the net income of a brand is multiplied to produce a brand's value. It is based on seven key factors: leadership, stability, market, internationality, trend, support and protection.

brand valuation The process of producing an estimate of the market value of a brand. There is some debate on and alternative methods of calculation but the real issue is whether or not any figures should be included on a company's balance sheet.

brand values The values and attributes associated with a specific brand. In a world where ever improving technology means it is easier to replicate functional characteristics and values, it is likely that emotional values will become increasingly important.

company brand A company that uses its name across a range of different brands, products and services. Also known as a *corporate brand.*

house brand Very similar to a company brand but it is possible that a *company brand* ranging across a variety of different sub-brands might not be a company in itself in which case technically it is a house brand.

manufacturer brand A product that has been produced and branded by its manufacturer.

product brand A brand based on one specific product but the type of brand most commonly imagined when the word brand is used.

range brand A brand that offers a range of different products and/or services across a number of different markets. Effectively they are product brands that have been brand extended.

retailer brand A brand whose primary business function is not in making but in selling products and services.

retailer's own brand Often know simply as *own-label* or *distributor's own brand* they are products and services produced by another company but sold under a retailer brand.

service brand A brand that offers a service to its consumers as opposed to a specific physical product.

sub-brand A product or service with added values that is endorsed by a company or house brand. It has the characteristics of a brand but in effect is branded twice once by its parent and once by itself.

superbrand The brand equivalent of a Hollywood superstar. A brand of significant stature that is universally recognisable and commands a committed following from a group of users.

umbrella brand Another name for a company or house brand which derives from the idea that the sub-brands, products and service all shelter under the protection of it.

Bibliography

Aaker D A, *Building Strong Brands* (1996) The Free Press.

Arnold D, *The Handbook of Brand Management* (1992) Century Business.

Baren M, *How it all Began* (1992) Smith Settle.

Baren M, *How it all Began – Up the High Street* (Special Edition 1996) printed for Past Times by Michael O'Mara Books Ltd.

Cooper A, *Brand Equity – A Lifestage Model* (January 1998) Ad Map.

Croft M, "Coca-Cola topples Marlboro as the world's most valuable brand" *Brand Strategy* (24 October 1997).

de Chernatory L & Dall'Olmo Riley F, "Branding in the service sector" *FT Mastering Management* No. 4 (September 1997).

Davidson J H, *Offensive Marketing* (1987) Penguin.

Davidson J H, *Even more Offensive Marketing* (1997) Penguin.

Dwek, R, "How far can brand extension be pushed?" *Campaign* (26 April 1996).

FitzGerald N, "Advertising for a successful Europe" (1997) Speech to the European Association of Advertising Agencies.

Godin, S, *Permission Marketing* (1999) Simon & Schuster.

Harding G & Walton P, *Bluff your Way in Marketing* (1987) Ravette Books Ltd.

Herzberg F, *Work and the Nature of Man* (1966) Williams Collins.

HHCL+Partners, "Marketing at a point of change" (1994).

Hine T, *The Total Package: the secret history and hidden meaning of boxes, bottles, cans and other persuasive containers* (1997) Back Bay Books; Little, Brown & Company.

Interbrand Brands, *An International Review* (1990) Mecury Business Books; Gold Arrow Publications Ltd.

King S, "What is a Brand?" (1970) Speech to the Advertising Association.

Klein, N, *No Logo* (2000) Flamingo.

Kotler P, *Marketing Management: Analysis, Planning and Control* (1996) Prentice-Hall.

Lasn, K, *Culture Jam: The Uncooling of America* (2000) Quill.

Levine, Locke, Searle & Weinberger, *The Cluetrain Manifesto* (2000) ft. com.

Marketing "Brand owning in the 21st Century" Leader Column (7 March 1996).

Maslow A H, *Motivation and Personality* (1954) Harper & Row.

Mihailovic & de Chernatony, "Brand bonding" *The Journal of Brand Management* (1994).

Mollerup P, *Marks of Excellence* (1997) Phaidon Press Ltd.

Olins W, *Corporate Identity* (1989) Thames & Hudson.

O'Sullivan T, "Branson is as Branson does" *Marketing Week* (14 October 1994).

Perrier R (ed.), *Interbrand Brand Valuation* (1997) Premier Books.

Perry Sir M, "The Brand: Vehicle for Value in a Changing Marketplace" (1994) Speech to the Advertising Association.

Pine, B J & Gilmore, J H, *The Experience Economy* (1999) Harvard Business School.

Richards A, "Brand new days" *Marketing* (4 December 1997).

Ries A & Trout J, *Positioning: The Battle for your Mind* (1981) McGraw-Hill.

Simpson E, "Brand wars" *Business Life Magazine* (November 1994).

Southgate P, *Total Branding by Design* (1994) Kogan Page.

Stiling M, *Famous Brand Names, Emblems and Trademarks*

(1980) David & Charles Ltd.

Trout, J & Rivkin S (Contributor), *Differentiate or Die* (2000) John Wiley & Sons.

Walton P, "Frankenstein and the meaning of life" (An examination of brand extension - paper (1988).

Walton P & Braun T, "Creating a language for innovation" (Unpublished paper 1996).

White, R, "Is the company brand the brand of the future?" *Admap* (May 1996).

Whitworth, M, "The image makers" *The Grocer* (10 December 1994).

Index